# space

# SPACE

RESHAPING YOUR HOME FOR THE WAY YOU WANT TO LIVE

## FAY SWEET

conran
OCTOPUS

First published in 1999 by

Conran Octopus Limited

a part of Octopus Publishing Group

2-4 Heron Quays

London E14 4JP


Reprinted in 2000, 2001

*Commissioning Editor*   Denny Hemming

*Managing Editor*   Catriona Woodburn

*Copy Editors*   Maxine McCaghy, Michelle Clark

*Indexer*   Hilary Bird

*Art Editors*   Tony Seddon, Alison Barclay

*Picture Researcher*   Clare Limpus

*Production Controller*   Sue Sharpless

British Library Cataloguing-in-Publication Data. A catalogue
record for this book is available from the British Library.
ISBN 1 84091 0437


Printed in China

# contents

# living spaces
## getting to where we are today

The home is a hothouse of ideas. Here we experiment with colour and texture, furnishings, lighting and room planning. But these are only a small part of the story. Often we're missing the real opportunities to make the most of our living environment, to make it more comfortable, dynamic and inspiring.

At no time have we been in such control of our domestic space. Though few of us may choose to design our own homes from scratch, and many of us live in older properties designed for an age that has long gone, we are nevertheless in great shape to adapt our living quarters to our modern life.

In the past, homes simply evolved in response to a variety of influences – to take an extreme example, people built sturdy manor houses and castles to keep themselves safe from the enemy. And sometimes it was social change that dictated the shape of housing – with the Industrial Revolution came the need to accommodate large numbers of people in the burgeoning towns, and the solution was the practical and space-saving terrace house. More recently the pressure on space in revived city centres and the changing nature of offices have led to an explosion of residential loft developments in what were once commercial buildings. The world changes. But never before have homeowners been so closely in charge of how their houses and apartments look and work; never have the possibilities been so great. Decorating provides superficial change, but more interesting and satisfying are three-dimensional architectural solutions.

7

# the modern home

The evolution of the modern house has taken a century to achieve. The pace and scale of change have been breathtaking. Most of us live in homes that benefit from the huge technological advances made during the past 100, or so, years. We take for granted the basics of shelter and warmth, fresh water and instant electricity; in addition to this we want a home that 'fits' us, that is sympathetic to, and supportive of, the way we live. We want a home that's a pleasure to be in, where we can store and display our possessions, a space that is beautiful and comfortable, safe and clean; a retreat that enhances our quality of life. It must also work in practical terms, according to our individual needs: family homes require plenty of child-friendly areas for safe play; those who enjoy cooking want generous preparation, cooking and dining space, and a home gym is irresistible to the enthusiastic athlete.

At the turn of the century, modern-thinking architects saw the opportunity to make new homes benefiting from the exciting new industrial age. In the 1920s the Swiss-born architect Le Corbusier expressed the idea that the home should be 'a machine for living in'. He was proposing not that the house should look high-tech and be filled with mechanical gadgets and exposed pipes, but that it should work with the economy, efficiency and elegance of a machine.

It is important to remember that at this time most of the Western world was still living in stuffy, dusty-cornered, heavily decorated and muffled nineteenth-century interiors. The idea that a home could be bright and open, easy-to-manage and filled with light, furniture and colour was shocking to many; but the world was changing fast. Electricity was just starting to come into widespread use in the home, and mechanical devices like the vacuum cleaner were new on the market (and frowned upon by many housewives who had spent much of their lives sweeping, scrubbing, washing and polishing the old way). Growing numbers of doctors and health visionaries promoted the benefits of sunlight and fresh air along with raised standards of hygiene, better food and exercise as a package of measures for improving health and quality of life. This was the birth of the twentieth century. Forward-thinking architects and designers became Modernist missionaries, preaching the gospel of the new age. Le Corbusier

LEFT  A rational and elegant modern interior with an ergonomically refined kitchen and an open stair to allow light to penetrate to the heart of the flat. Yet this is not a 1990s loft, but one of the beautiful apartments that make up Le Corbusier's *Unité d'habitation* in Marseille, completed in 1952.

RIGHT  One of the great visionaries of the 20th century, Le Corbusier's ideas about urban living are as fresh and valid as ever. This modern space is modelled on Le Corbusier's famous housing block. It is light and airy, ideal for busy urban dwellers, clutter-free, and easy-to-clean and maintain.

ABOVE Pale, open and bathed in natural light, this sitting room at The Hill House, with its obvious Japanese influences, was completed by Charles Rennie Mackintosh in 1903. This modern masterpiece marks a defining moment in the history of house design; we see the shutters closing on the 19th century and the glimmers of emerging Modernism. The simplicity of this room would have been breathtaking at the time.

was among those who were quick to appreciate and interpret the changing mood. His radical, plain, box-like villas and apartments, with their huge picture windows, sun decks and flat roofs, were conceived to suit those people who wanted to break from the grim and grubby past and join a new world where machines and technology would liberate man from drudgery.

In an era that witnessed the development of the liner, the aeroplane and the car, Le Corbusier saw that the clarity and rationality of

these designs could be adapted to the house. He admired the precision and calculation of the engineer who 'achieves harmony' and he recognized that the engineer's skill was in understanding a problem and solving it as efficiently as possible. The sleek shape of the ship, plane or car was designed to ensure its optimum passage through water, air or on the road. In the Modernist phrase, 'form followed function'. Corbusier employed a similar approach. Starting with the problem – how to

accommodate a modern lifestyle – he set out to provide a living space to fit. Like the best architects, he spent time understanding how the occupants might use their home and identifying how to meet their needs, and then he tailor-made a house to fit. This approach has been used by some of the world's most successful designers of one-off homes. Scotland's Charles Rennie Mackintosh, who at the very start of the twentieth century was among the first to create all-white, light-flooded interiors, spent a great

ABOVE **The white room today. This space is so elegant, it has the aura of a serene sculpture. Partitions denote separate areas without disturbing the open-plan design.**

deal of time with his clients, visiting their existing homes before setting to work on the bespoke designs.

Despite the rudimentary communications of the early 1900s, the new ideas lit architectural imaginations worldwide. In Scandinavia, Alvar Aalto was among those experimenting with stripped-back shapes and plans, the Bauhaus design school in Germany blended art with technology to make the functional beautiful, and in the USA Frank Lloyd Wright bust open the box and made open-plan spaces to reflect the informal American lifestyle.

However, Le Corbusier also understood that 'architecture goes beyond utilitarian needs'. The best domestic architecture also includes

spaces which allow us to recharge and to be tranquil. A home should contain elements of delight, and most of all, of beauty. This may be achieved in any number of ways: by a particularly fine window, proportions that feel instantly right, a window seat in a quiet corner or even a panel of stained glass.

After a century of Modernism, we are now ready to leave behind our nostalgia for the imagined past and embrace the beauty of simple, functional design. This doesn't mean we must sacrifice comfort or reject decoration, it simply means that we can learn the lessons of the past without apeing it, and appreciate what the present can offer. While commissioning a one-off house

remains a luxury, it is clearly within our reach to shape our homes to better accommodate the way we want to live in them today.

ABOVE One marked trend in contemporary housing design, particularly in apartments, has been to remove walls completely and open up spaces. We no longer want to live our lives in a series of separate and formal room compartments, but prefer communal, multi-purpose areas.

LEFT The medieval hall-house was one of the earliest prototypes of open-plan living. During this century, American architect Frank Lloyd Wright reinterpreted this idea and, here at Fallingwater, produced flexible living spaces which served as dining room, library and sitting room all rolled into one.

# our changing needs

Alongside new ideas in architecture, the modern home has been shaped by factors such as changing social and economic patterns. During the past 200 years, the single biggest impact on living patterns in industrialized countries has been the population drift away from rural areas to urban centres. Ways had to be devised to accommodate this vast influx of people within easy reach of their work. In addition to the growth in urban living, household sizes are shrinking – in the Western

BELOW With the growing demand for urban housing, developers and architects have striven towards making the most of our space and creating more interesting homes. A large lightwell has opened up this once-redundant roof space and transformed it into a sunny, inviting living area.

world at the turn of the twentieth century the average household size was around four-and-a-half people, today this has dropped to two.

In the last two decades we have experienced new changes that are affecting housing patterns. More people are living alone – we are leaving home earlier, marrying later, divorcing more frequently, living longer and, indeed, growing numbers of us are simply choosing

LEFT **This modern flat is carved from a large nineteenth-century house. This house would originally have been used by one family and its staff, but today it is too large for most families and has been converted into smaller dwellings to serve the growing number of one- and two-person households.**

urban land prices increased and the cost of housing escalated. Following the post-war boom in property ownership, the home has now become our most valuable personal asset, a status symbol even, and one on which we are prepared to lavish enormous amounts of time and money. The house is now seen as an expression of our taste and as an extension of our personality. It's a sophisticated language, but one we all understand.

Another factor that has been brought to bear on housing is the relative informality of our modern lifestyle, which has changed how we think about and use interiors. A nineteenth-century family would hardly recognize how its town house is used by the property's modern owners. Households then, of even a modest income, employed a maid or two; fires needed constant tending; coal was carried through the house from the cellar; lighting was by gas or candle; food was prepared on a range, usually in the basement; there was a best reception room for receiving guests; and the family parlour almost certainly contained a piano as the focus of

family entertainment. Today the basement is more likely to have been knocked through to make a big family kitchen and dining area, the reception room and parlour are probably one long room where the television tends to dominate; and there is no need for maids when the house has central heating and electricity.

Of all rooms, the kitchen has experienced the most dramatic reinvention during the course of this century, brought about by the full force of social, technological and design changes. Except in the poorest of homes, this basement or ground-floor room was once the domain of the housewife and her staff, and was used solely for the preparation and cooking of family meals. Until the last war, the family's children would rarely be seen here and the man of the house would have no reason at all to visit this domestic engine room. In the immediate post-war years, domestic staff were replaced by electric, labour-saving appliances. By the 1960s and 1970s, the kitchen was transformed into a super hygienic laboratory, fitted from

to live alone. This change in social patterns is, of course, having an impact on the housing market, with more flats and smaller homes being built to accommodate the single homeowner.

The economic factors at play in housing are equally significant and are linked to this constantly changing social picture. As towns and cities grew in size in the early part of the twentieth century, so

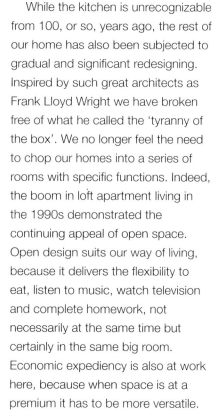

wall-to-wall and from ceiling-to-floor with matching, wipe-clean Melamine units and equipped with a full battery of plug-in electrical equipment. Even so it remained the wife's domain, dedicated to the task of preparing and cooking the daily meals. By the end of the century, however, the kitchen has changed again. It is now the very hub of family life, a versatile, welcoming space that is used for cooking, washing, playing, eating, homework, DIY and, quite unthinkable a century ago, even for entertaining guests.

While the kitchen is unrecognizable from 100, or so, years ago, the rest of our home has also been subjected to gradual and significant redesigning. Inspired by such great architects as Frank Lloyd Wright we have broken free of what he called the 'tyranny of the box'. We no longer feel the need to chop our homes into a series of rooms with specific functions. Indeed, the boom in loft apartment living in the 1990s demonstrated the continuing appeal of open space. Open design suits our way of living, because it delivers the flexibility to eat, listen to music, watch television and complete homework, not necessarily at the same time but certainly in the same big room. Economic expediency is also at work here, because when space is at a premium it has to be more versatile.

The process of change in the home is often slow and subtle, but it is continuous. New factors are affecting the shape, look and function of the building. For example, ecological concerns and pressures demand that we address how our lifestyles affect the planet. Can we reduce our energy and water consumption? Can we make better use of natural energy? Can we recycle our waste more efficiently? There is now a whole movement in design to try and find new ways to use sustainable construction materials and to make homes more energy efficient. We also want to know how buildings can be made to

BELOW The first fitted kitchens were a terrifying array of units and electrical appliances, all of which were put proudly on display. Their gleaming, scrubbed-down, laboratory whiteness proclaimed that these were spotless, hygienic places that produced food and clean clothes for the family. This housewife was a well-equipped 'professional' and would certainly have been the envy of her suburban friends.

adapt to changing family patterns; and how to house a population with an increasing proportion of old people. These may sound like issues to be tackled by the policy makers and housebuilders, but they apply to all of us as we try to make a home which is adaptable, ecologically efficient, and safe and comfortable for our old age.

ABOVE This contemporary kitchen is understated, elegant and sculptural. With the fusion of kitchen and living space, kitchen design now follows less traditional lines because it has to match other furnishings. This is a kitchen you would not want to hide away.

# homes today

Most homes perform a wide range of functions. The best allow us to live together as families and separately as individuals, and can embrace the variety of activities that make up our lives. Lifestyles evolve constantly, and homes need to adapt accordingly.

The home is such a familiar concept to us that we rarely take the time to think about why the rooms are arranged in a particular way and how we use space. In fact, to meet their changing needs, every generation slightly alters what has gone before. In medieval times in Northern Europe, the main room, or hall, was often the only room of the house. (We're talking about the homes of the rich, of course. If you were poor you probably lived in a stone, mud and turf hut.) It was in this hall that people met, kept warm, talked, ate and even slept. Nobility sat and ate shoulder-to-shoulder with the rest of their household. Over the centuries the hall-house was gradually chopped into separate rooms, each with its own distinct function. First a screen was erected across one end by the entrance door – this stopped draughts, but also separated the food storage, preparation and cooking areas from the rest of the space. Then, as greater privacy and comfort were sought by the master – at the end of the hall where he and his family and favoured men ate – a room was made for them to withdraw into. This withdrawing room was also called the parlour – from the French *parler*, to talk. Later a chamber was added above, which contained the master's bed. This space also provided privacy for the family and acted as a private meeting room for the master. (A room used solely for sleeping in is a fairly recent concept, dating from the eighteenth century.) In modern times the hall, where it exists at all, has been relegated to a small lobby area around the front and back door.

The story of the division of the hall-house gives us clues to understanding how we make buildings adapt to the way we like to live. We enjoy open space, but still like to inhabit a mixture of private and social space. Some areas will be full of activity while others will be small oases of quiet, created to provide space for reading and thinking. To accommodate all these needs, the structure must contain different types of spaces: from the public space of the doorstep and front door, to the semi-public space of the hallway and perhaps kitchen, to the most private space of all – the bedroom.

LEFT **This sheet of stretched canvas marks a subtle yet clear division between the social space of the living area and the more private sleeping quarters.**

RIGHT **This converted industrial building is the height of modernity, but it still borrows the conventions of traditional housing design to denote the hierarchy of spaces. The freestanding screen-wall situated by the door creates a lobby or hall. Although it is a minimal structure, it is substantial enough to effectively inhibit the visitor and prevent him from marching straight into the heart of the apartment.**

# semi-public space

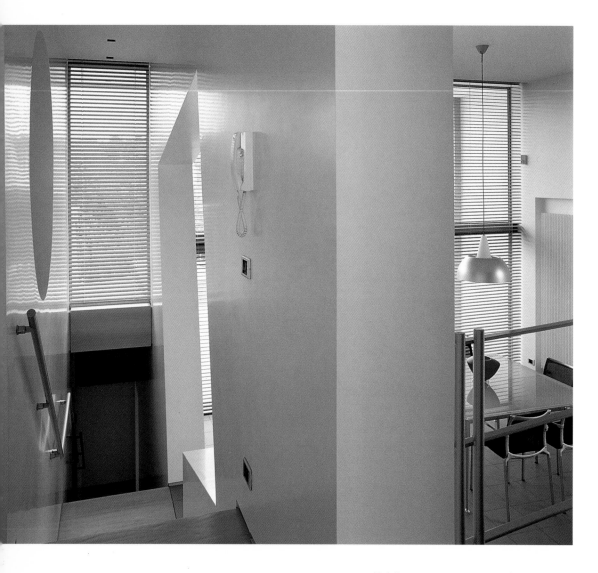

ABOVE  Once you have opened the front door, the hall is used as a holding space to accept special deliveries or talk to callers you don't know well. The more private areas of the home, such as the dining room, are out of sight and are decorated in far more exuberant colours.

RIGHT  As a space used for storage of items like overcoats, wellingtons and bicycles, the hall often has to be given more durable finishes than the rest of the house. This part-glazed screen allows in welcome light and maintains a greater sense of space in the living room than would a solid wall.

Public space stops at our doorstep. The threshold marks an extremely important invisible line over which only family and friends and invited visitors may pass. This line is understood and respected by just about everyone – even regular house visitors, like the postman and electricity-meter readers, will not cross the threshold unless invited to do so. To feel comfortable at this sensitive meeting point, and in order that conversations can be conducted observing these boundaries, we have developed a threshold and hallway, with standing space both inside and out.

Security is, of course, an issue, particularly in towns where we may feel safer if the front of the property opens on to a public thoroughfare. In blocks of apartments, electronic surveillance helps in selecting who we allow into the property. We need our refuge from the world outside, we need escape from the pressures of work, we need to know that we are secure at home.

After the first expression of personality offered by a front door and its approach, the space inside the front door, even in the most flamboyant of homes, tends to be fairly neutral. It is usually finished in hardwearing materials that you will not find anywhere else in the home. This is semi-public space, designated as a holding or transitional area where we may accept deliveries, rest empty bottles before they are taken to the recycling bin, or store a bicycle. This is often screened from the rest of the home, making it clear to callers that they only pass further into the home with the permission of the householder. We are so familiar with the hierarchy of space within the home that the barriers that mark this transitional public/private space do not even have to have solid walls. Often glass bricks, or a tall sideboard or bookcase will be sufficient to suggest the boundaries between the public and private areas.

# social space

BELOW It was unthinkable even a couple of generations ago to entertain guests in the kitchen. Today it is commonplace, and we are even happy to have the kitchen on display from the sitting room. However, this design allows for the living area to be separated off by sliding the doors across.

Most of us have become so accustomed to inviting friends into our homes and offering hospitality, that we hardly stop to think about what we are doing. At a basic level, inviting someone into your home is a way of demonstrating the type of friendship you share. It indicates that you are happy to reveal something of your personal life, and trust that person to enter your private domain.

While we invite people into the home more often than previous

generations, most occasions are unlikely to be very formal. When considering what sort of space you would like to inhabit, it is crucial to assess how it will be used. For example, until quite recently standard family houses were built with a separate dining room. The table would be laid with condiments and cutlery, and three times a day, at fixed, regular meal times, the family would be called to sit and eat. Nowadays our lives are rarely that

regulated and predictable. People eat breakfast at a breakfast bar, or at a kitchen table; if we go out to work we don't come home for lunch, and supper is often a fairly informal meal taken at the kitchen table or seated in front of the television. Not surprisingly, few people want to devote an entire room to a table and chairs used for formal dining.

A separate dining room has gradually become a defunct space, unused except for special occasions. Our first response to this waste was to take down the wall that divided the dining room from the kitchen. The merging of cooking and eating into one area is a popular choice and it is almost inconceivable in most homes that we will ever again see the separation of the two. However, remodelling doesn't finish there; we now have a new impulse. The delight of dining alfresco has meant that even in chilly northern climes we want to simulate the experience of taking our meals outdoors. We have begun to remove the barrier between the garden and the interior of the house, whether it be through the addition of a conservatory or the replacement of a solid wall with a transparent one. New advances in the production of glass and tough, lightweight fabrics have made this transparency an exciting possibility and one that is not just the province of high-cost, cutting-edge architecture projects.

Along with sharing food with friends and family, our homes need to be able to cope with other sorts of social occasions – from children's birthday parties and formal dinner engagements to inviting a group of friends to watch big sporting events on television. Once again, Frank Lloyd Wright's ideas about the flexible open-plan living area have proved to suit the demands of modern life. One large living space is now a highly desirable element in both houses and flats.

ABOVE  **Even in reasonably formal homes we enjoy the sense of open space. Here a wall has been removed between the living and dining areas to provide an internal vista as well as great views right through the house into the garden.**

# work space

Increasing numbers of us are working full time, or part of the time, from home and so a quiet, private area is often a requirement. Most of us don't have the luxury of space that allows us to dedicate an entire room to an office, but with forward planning and ingenuity a work space can be incorporated into most homes. A key element is a large worksurface with plenty of storage space above and below. Telephone and power sockets are also needed. Sometimes a small work area can be built into the corner of a bedroom or living room, and generous shelving and cupboard space here will ensure that the office doesn't spread into the rest of the room. For more space, an attic might be converted to provide an extra room. Work areas have to be created in such a way that one feels encouraged to go and use them. The availability of natural light and the way that artificial light falls on the area is of vital importance, and so too is a sense of order and calm generated by the decoration and layout of that space. Too often the work space is crammed into an area below the stairs, or in a mean corner of a room. Good planning and detailing can even enable the incorporation of a work

ABOVE  A variety of ingenious schemes have been devised to incorporate a work area into the living space. The balance must be struck to create a space that is good to work in and avoids dominating the living area. The home office, above, can be closed off at the end of the day using sliding screens.

RIGHT  This narrow slot of an office makes efficient use of the space available. One appealing detail is the internal window, which allows a view into the living space. Once again the desk and shelving area can be hidden from view, this time by an enormous blonde wood sliding panel.

space into the main area of a room, so that it can be a positive addition, not an unsightly and unwelcome distraction. Instead of thinking of a poky corner desk, why not consider a beautiful slab of slate that runs the whole length of the room? Think of your working equipment as objects to be arranged; books, files, a computer, all possess some beauty and character.

It requires concentration and discipline to work at home, so it is often psychologically effective to be able to 'travel' to work – an attic is ideal because it means that you are away from the parts of the house associated with leisure hours. However, other rooms work just as effectively when there

ABOVE A home office or work area does not have to be hidden away from sight. This cosy, informal work space is an intrinsic part of the surrounding room. This desk with a view has a sweeping countertop which continues around the room as a useful breakfast bar and shelf.

is a door to close or some other way of marking off the area from distractions. Home offices can be sited in the most ingenious places: built into a cupboard or corridor, say, or constructed as a suspended platform. A platform built over a deep stairwell, in order to make the most of the previously unused ceiling void at the head of the staircase, is a highly inventive use of space.

# personal space

Along with spending time together in the home and learning social skills, we all need time to ourselves. Safe, flexible play space is a must for young children. Even if you have a garden, children still need some room inside that is their own. In recent years, designers and architects have turned their attentions to this important, but previously under-considered function of the home and have come up with solutions which are separate, colourful and fun. In a house, it is likely that the best site for a play space is on the ground floor, where children can be watched. However, children need to be able to develop on their own and so a play area will need to be free of precious adult possessions and any items that can cause damage or be damaged.

Children's bedrooms are also important places to encourage independence, and the ability to play and work alone. By pursuing their own interests they are given the freedom to develop their characters. Many children's bedrooms have evolved into multifunctional spaces; the raised bed has become a ubiquitous solution to providing storage, desk, play and sleeping space in even the smallest of rooms.

As children get older, their desire for autonomy grows – the teenager's bedroom is an essential place for self-expression and rebellion. A real bonus in many larger homes is a mini apartment/bedsit which can be created for teenagers in preparation

ABOVE **This is an extreme interpretation of securing your own personal space. This vast loft area contains small simple room-cubes, each like a monk's cell, for privacy. Each cube is dedicated to particular activities and is used by both parents and children.**

RIGHT **We all need room to play, and for grown-ups that usually means pursuing hobbies. In this home a storage system was devised to contain the accoutrements of home entertainment which would otherwise clutter up the space.**

for independence and leaving home. These are places where teenagers can invite friends, even prepare meals, but still remain safely under the family roof. (It's worth remembering that this type of accommodation is also ideal for elderly relatives who want to maintain their independence but who, perhaps, no longer wish to live in a whole house of their own. For older people you may need to address the additional issues of access, and so a converted attic may be great for a teenager but less than ideal for their grandparents.)

Grown-ups need their own recreational areas too – interests like playing a musical instrument, listening to music, painting or photography, all add to our quality of life and sense of fulfilment. These can be accommodated with creative space manipulation. This is precisely

RIGHT **An ordinary basement lightwell has been transformed into a fantasy beach using large pebbles, coastal grasses and a violet-blue wall. By folding back the entire glass door/wall, this bedroom becomes a restful daytime space for reading or working.**

FAR RIGHT **A slim wall slotted into the centre of this bedroom gives privacy to the two children who sleep here. They each have a raised bed with lots of storage underneath for clothes and toys. The bed boxes free up floor space to make more room for playing.**

the challenge that stimulates us to think about how best to use our rooms, particularly areas like the bedroom that remain empty through most of the daytime.

Along with space to play, we all need space to be quiet and separate from the rest of the household. Here the bedroom can provide an ideal place to read, write letters or concentrate on homework and other projects without distraction. In the past, this room has tended to be one of the most underused spaces in the house, given over just to a bed and the storage of clothes. Where space in a home is limited, we can learn from the multiple functions served by the average child's bedroom. As already discussed, a bedroom is one of the obvious places for a home office, but even if you don't work at home it's a good place to accommodate a desk and computer. For children and adults alike, the bedroom can provide important personal space where it is possible to take a break from the pressures of the day, and take time to be quiet and uninterrupted.

# shaping space

## opening up and defining spaces

LEFT AND ABOVE A really neat solution to screening off the kitchen. Two enormous sliding panels are used to dramatically alter the tone of this dining space. In the main picture there are clear views to the food preparation area and to the garden beyond. However, when a more formal and secluded feel is wanted in the space, the blue panel can be slid across and the noise, smells and distractions of the kitchen disappear.

f we want to be imaginative in shaping our homes to fit our lives, we must first understand the fundamentals involved in manipulating space. How do we open up our homes? How can we welcome in more natural light? Is it possible to define spaces in different ways? This section of the book provides an insight into the techniques used by architects and designers to shape and mould interior spaces.

There are many ways of achieving more and better space and the choice you make depends on the style of your home, the extent of the change you would like to make and the size of your budget.

The most frequent approach to opening up space is simply to knock down internal walls. In many schemes this can be the ideal solution, but before you take such a radical step it is worth considering some other, less obvious and perhaps more inventive options.

The first question to ask yourself is what you hope to achieve. Do you actually need more space or do you simply want to reduce your household clutter and create the illusion of more space? Would letting in more natural light help to open up an area? Can you identify any dead areas in your home that would provide you with interesting places for expansion? Do you want to make better use of the space you already have or do you plan to create additional space? Consider as many options as you can, then be clear about your objectives from the start, and your finished scheme will give you greater long-term pleasure.

# opening up space

More space and open space is what we all desire, and this is where creative thinking can produce stunning results. New materials for better insulation and efficient heating systems mean that we no longer need to be surrounded and encumbered by thick, solid walls for warmth and protection. We now have access to materials and building technologies that are truly liberating and which enable us to open up our homes as never before.

To create an inspiring, visually stimulating and comfortable living environment we are constantly developing ways to shape space. We can use slender sliding walls to add flexibility to rooms, beams to dispense with solid walls, and light and colour to enhance our environment. By using our ingenuity to discover potential in even the most unpromising corners we have the power to shape our homes to suit the way we live.

LEFT In many older, modest family houses, rooms were small. A more formal lifestyle demanded different rooms for different functions and small rooms were practical to heat. Central heating and an informal lifestyle have helped give us the freedom to open up spaces. The positions of old walls are clearly evident in this top-floor apartment. Quite unlike our ancestors we like to show off our kitchen and enjoy living in an open space which incorporates cooking, dining and watching television.

RIGHT Clever design and engineering combine to make this highly space-efficient spiral staircase. Glass treads ensure maximum light penetration from above.

# creating the illusion

ABOVE  This long hallway is finished in pale colours to enhance the sense of space. The use of mirrors on the cupboard doors reflects light and creates the illusion of space.

ABOVE RIGHT  By simplifying this room, stripping floors, removing fancy cornicing, and painting panelling around the window the same colour as the walls, the room feels taller and wider.

FAR RIGHT  Flush fitting, floor-to-ceiling cupboard doors provide storage space and a low-impact plain backdrop. Panelled doors would be much more visually intrusive.

Where you want to experiment with decorative solutions that open up space, the key is to keep things simple: limit the number of colours and materials used in a room and reduce its visual 'noise'.

A greater sense of space can be achieved in almost any home by simply tidying away clutter. Is every cupboard stacked efficiently and every corner and corridor put to good use? Few of us could honestly claim to be that organized, yet an important starting point for maximizing space is to incorporate generous storage areas. Once clutter is reduced, there is a streamlining effect which generates a greater sense of space. Lining a wall from floor to ceiling with cupboards allows a huge volume of possessions to be hidden away. However, deep cupboards will eat into the floor space in small rooms, so try to keep the cupboards shallow.

The materials and colours you use will also have an effect. As a general rule, darker shades, soft textures and pattern will seem to close in a space while smooth, reflective, light-coloured finishes will appear to open it up. Remember that painting large fittings, such as cupboard doors, the same colour as the walls will reduce their impact on the room.

If you live in an older property it is likely to be finished with decorative skirting and moulded cornicing. These can be attractive (and may be protected in a listed building), but they add visual complexity to a room and give the appearance of closing in the space. Removing these altogether, or replacing them with much simpler finishes, will create the illusion of a larger and more open area.

Boosting light levels really enhances a room's openness. By using artificial light, exciting effects can be created by washing entire walls with up- and downlighters or by highlighting particular room features (see page 66).

Strategically placed mirrors can reflect more natural light. An intriguing double vista can be created if you have a window close to a corner of a room and can fix a sheet of mirror glass at right angles to the window; however, in most cases the most effective use of a mirror is to place it opposite the main window where it draws sunlight to the far wall and then sends back a soft spread of reflected light.

# removing internal walls

One of the major problems caused by poor conversions, where a space has been chopped up thoughtlessly, is a lasting lack of cohesion. A skilled architect can bring unity to a series of dislocated areas and produce an elegant, logical solution. You will gain much from employing an architect and talking through their suggestions, but remember that at the end of the day you will be living in the space, and so it is important to consider your own solutions too.

ABOVE **This space contains sitting, dining and kitchen areas. Without walls the continuous, open-plan space feels open and light. Chopped into rooms, it would seem very claustrophobic.**

At its most dramatic, the removal of all internal walls will certainly open out a space, but it won't necessarily produce great results. An entirely open area can lack interest and subtlety, and you may end up living with a very oddly proportioned single room. For safety reasons you will also need to take professional advice before removing walls, and those performing an important structural role may have to stay *in situ* or be replaced by beams.

The most effective results are usually achieved with creative thinking and often quite minimal disruption. Removing just part of a wall between two rooms can prove a better solution than wholesale demolition. Another often successful idea is to incorporate corridors into the living space. Not only will this add significantly to the room size, but it can also enhance the quality of the entire house or apartment by dispensing with a gloomy passageway.

OVERLEAF **Removing walls and using a limited palette of materials produce interiors of breathtaking calm and almost monastic simplicity, providing a welcome respite from everyday pressures. Le Corbusier would certainly approve of the lack of clutter.**

BELOW **A great open space, filled with light and with inviting views over the garden. Even the staircase has been melted away to this minimal yet striking flight of treads suspended in space by fine wires. The long kitchen counter and dining table encourage us into the open room.**

# attics, basements and cellars

An exciting way of opening up space is to expand into previously unused and neglected 'dead' areas, such the roof or basement.

High ceilings have a huge visual impact and therefore a room set under the roof can be transformed if the ceiling is removed, allowing the space to soar up to the rafters. Glass panels in the ceiling or rooflights will also enhance the effect.

If you are lucky enough to have a very large attic space, the possibility of creating an extra room or two exists. The key to putting this plan into action is a roof construction that doesn't eat into, or completely obstruct, the space; in most houses this is fine, but some modern houses are built with trusses that criss-cross the roof space making it almost impossible to open up. If this is the case, why not open up the room below and enjoy the extra room height.

At the bottom of the house you may be able to extend downwards and reclaim space from a cellar or basement. It is always advisable to seek professional advice before undertaking such work. A deep space might be transformed to make an extra bathroom or a home gym. It may be possible to excavate shallow cellars to provide a useful standing-height room. For a more dramatic use of the space, a cellar can be incorporated into the room above to make an unusual double-height living or kitchen space.

ABOVE LEFT  Basements in older houses were often large, and plenty remain in use as store rooms. With imaginative thought such areas can be incorporated into daily use.This basement provides kitchen and dining space. Light is drawn in by windows that have been extended downwards from the first floor.

LEFT  A quite brilliant solution to bringing more light into attic rooms. Strip off the tiled roof and replace it with a strong metal frame filled with glazed panels. This has made a really wonderful bedroom.

ABOVE  One of the best ways to introduce light into the top floors of a building is to fit huge rooflights that flood the area with natural light and can provide useful fresh-air ventillation on warm days.

# external glass walls

RIGHT **This dining area is given more room to breathe by replacing a small window with an entire wall of glass. The white wall beyond screens off an unattractive view, and the wall serves the additional purpose of reflecting precious light back into the room.**

BELOW **Delicious dappled light is drawn into this bathroom, where darkness used to reign behind a solid brick wall. The new glass wall has opened the space and introduced life with the changing patterns of light.**

RIGHT **In all areas of our home we are increasingly interested in blurring the boundaries between inside and out; whole sliding glass walls leading to a small terrace give this narrow bedroom a more generous and airier feel.**

FAR RIGHT **In the past the corridor has been an unloved but practical means of passing from one space to another. By adding windows and rooflights the narrow space is drenched in light and walking its length becomes an event.**

Increasing natural lightfall is a great way of opening up rooms and making them feel more spacious. An effective way of drawing more light into a home is to enlarge the windows and doors, and the most dramatic approach to this is to replace the whole of an existing external wall with a huge sheet of glass. There is something undeniably thrilling about glass that stretches from floor to ceiling and wall to wall: an enormous unbroken window on the outside.

While we enjoy the protection and refuge provided by the home, we still want to see the street, the garden and the stars. We desire a connection with the world beyond our window. In our search for more space, there is constant experiment in dissolving the barriers between inside and out.

In the 1940s, Modernist architect Mies van der Rohe designed the

weight and withstand heavy knocks. Large sheets can be used as double, or even triple, glazing for protection against the extremes of hot and cold weather, and although a home with glass walls may feel vulnerable to intruders, toughened glass can allay these fears and provide as much protection as traditional solid walls.

If you are considering removing a whole external wall, the price is likely to be a deciding factor. Single, wall-size sheets will certainly be expensive, and a more cost-effective solution may be to opt for a frame divided into large glazed sections. Certainly this will suit a scheme at garden or terrace level, where a wall made of folding or sliding doors will appear to dissolve away. Another option is to use glass bricks. The thick, pebbly glass creates a subtle, dappled effect as the light filters through.

Farnsworth House – a large glass box of a building. This single-storey rectangular pavilion, with great glass panels as external walls, has only one solid enclosure – the bathroom area – at its centre. Indeed, throughout the twentieth century architects have striven for increased transparency in their constructions, and have been supported in their aims by the improved technology of glass manufacturing. So advanced are today's techniques that glass can be produced in vast sheets that are strong enough to bear considerable

# internal walls

BELOW When it's neither practical nor desirable to remove an internal wall, interest is added and light drawn through by piercing the structure. Here, along with two doorways, the wall has been opened up to provide a wonderfully eye-catching fireplace.

We have become so familiar with some aspects of our homes that it can be difficult to spot opportunities and think afresh about them. Internal walls can be a very dull affair – solid partitions to designate areas aren't much to get excited about. However, with some creative thinking, walls can be a positive contribution to the space. If you choose to keep your traditional solid walls, some very clever effects can be created by punching holes through them. Internal windows perform a number of functions: they allow light to flow through the building; they can create stunning vistas through the space; and, if made in intriguing shapes such as horizontal slots or circles, they add a sculptural element to a room. Some of the cleverest internal windows can frame a view so perfectly that we are unsure if we are we looking at a window or a picture. Even a window as small as 250 millimetres (10 inches) square can make a significant visual impact on a room and if it doesn't let through

LEFT  Sliding doors and panels take up minimal floor space but provide all the privacy of a solid fixed wall. Unlike conventional walls they allow an area to be opened up or closed off according to need. When made of opaque glass, they also allow natural light to pass through.

BELOW  Pierced walls are ideal for adding visual interest to a room. As well as framing a view they can be used as a decorative surround for single objects like a vase or sculpture. Pierced walls allow pockets of light to filter into an area, helping to dispel any feelings of claustrophobia.

huge quantities of light, it will still give the illusion of adding openness.

Replacing internal walls with glazed ones will bring in additional light and will enhance the sense of an open space whilst maintaining some sound-insulation. It is a good idea to consult with an architect or builder before taking a hammer to your own wall, as you may dangerously weaken the structure. In some instances you may be required to glaze an internal opening in order to comply with fire regulations.

# atriums and glass stairs

BELOW  The atrium is a device used in countless huge modern office buildings as a way of drawing light into the core of the structure. They are a luxury in most homes because usually we prefer to have the extra floor space. However, as you can see here, even a small atrium can lighten up the centre of a building and introduce a luxurious sense of light and space.

RIGHT  The stairwell provides a great opportunity to draw light through a building. This is particularly effective when a generous rooflight is combined with glass balustrading, but the whole effect is magical when the stairs themselves are also built in glass.

OVERLEAF  Where light is drawn into every part of the building, it opens up the possibilities of using space in different ways. This large landing would once just have been circulation space but now it has been transformed into an attractive dining area.

Rooflights have in the past been rather a drab affair – mean windows obscured by grime, allowing in little more than a dribble of light. However, in recent years homes have seen rather more dramatic interventions from above, as domestic designers have borrowed from their commercial property colleagues to make the most of direct overhead light. Of course the quality of this light varies through the day, but it is a very welcome supplement to buildings in dense urban neighbourhoods where lightfall through windows can often be obscured by surrounding buildings. Light from above also has the added appeal of being unexpected.

The most popular way of drawing light through the roof is the addition of skylights, and here technology has advanced to make larger and larger panels. Even more exciting are off-the-shelf glazed domes, which can introduce wonderful pools of light. To bring that precious light right through the building, architects have employed a range of devices including the sinking of glass panels into floors and the removal of whole sections of floors, in a smaller-scale version of the office-block atrium.

One of the most effective routes to bring light down through a building is via the stairwell. The greater the openness of the stair the better the quality of the light, and so in many projects solid balustrades are replaced with glass panels, and in the most thrilling, even the stairs themselves are constructed in glass.

# extensions

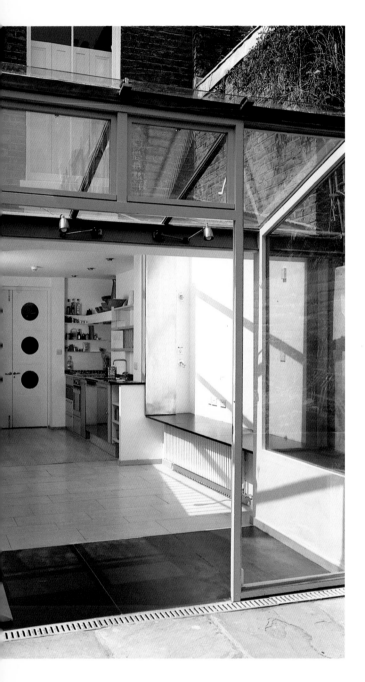

Extensions provide some of the most exciting opportunities to break free from the boundaries of a traditional brick-built room. There is no need to opt for the ubiquitous conservatory-style add-on either. During the past decade the extension has been constantly revisited and reinvented by architects, and because extensions are often small and don't always require planning permission, the results are infinitely varied.

Many designers are exploring ways of increasing transparency by reducing the presence of a structure. The advances in glass technology and the skills of the architect have even combined to produce a frame-free, all-glass extension. In these, massive panels of glass have been made strong enough to support the weight of horizontal panels laid on top to form a roof.

Of course, not all extensions have to be wholly transparent in order to maximize space; other options include a simple garden room with a solid roof, or perhaps a pavilion on stilts, a glass pyramid, or even a nylon, tented structure.

The skill in achieving an enhanced sense of openness is not only to draw in plenty of light, but also to manage skilfully the transition to the outside. Boundaries can be blurred in many ways, including continuing floor finishes, benches and counters through the space to the outside and by painting exterior walls the same colour as interior ones.

ABOVE The extension is the most popular way of adding living space to the home. In recent years architects have devised brilliant design solutions which don't just add space, but also improve the rest of the house. Here the boundary between inside and out is blurred by the slender-framed structure.

LEFT This extension is a glazed pavilion sitting high up above the city rooftops. Big slabs of glass give uninterrupted views and the solid flat roof provides protection from the direct glare of the sun.

ABOVE A really clever way of drawing light into the house, this exciting, reclining wall-size window allows light into the first floor and into the basement.

# defining space

Although we may want our home to have the advantages of open-planning, with its generosity of space and light, we still feel the need to delineate areas and create order in that space. A single living area can accommodate many activities, but few of us want to see everything happening at once. For example, to focus the mind and provide privacy, most of us would prefer a home office to be separated from dining or cooking areas. Any well-planned home has to provide for the times when we need to be alone and quiet, as well as those times when we want to enjoy the company of family and friends.

While walls are the obvious solution for marking out different areas, these permanent fixtures consume space and can block precious light. In contemporary housing, a variety of different methods have evolved to mark off and define spaces. Lightweight and translucent screens and freestanding units can act as room dividers, while an even more subtle delineation can be achieved by changes in flooring levels, and the use of different colours and materials.

LEFT **By embracing the bed, low-level walls mark off this raised sleeping area. By not using full-height walls, the room remains filled with natural sunlight.**

RIGHT **A half-height partition marks off the raised kitchen from the sitting area and adds interest with its subtle panelled pattern.**

# partitions and dividers

We have become ever more inventive in the ways we define our living space, and a great deal of this effort has been spent on reinventing the humble wall. In most homes where space and natural light are at a premium, the solid, floor-to-ceiling wall has a limited role in dividing up the interior. We have turned instead to the partition, waist-high counter or wall and the multi-purpose room divider to separate spaces.

The low-level wall/counter is often all that is required to mark out an area. We have become so sophisticated at understanding the visual language of the built environment that we know at a glance what purpose this fulfils. Where there is sufficient room, a wide unit can double up as storage and display space, and in a kitchen it will also provide a work counter and a housing for kitchen appliances.

The straight line is direct and efficient, but don't feel restricted to using that alone; curved partitions, low-level walls, and dividers of varying height add interest to a room. A gentle crescent shape can be used to 'embrace' a portion of space, perhaps to create a separate dining 'room' or soft seating area, while a long, undulating serpentine wall can create the optical illusion of lengthening a room. A single curve is soft, informal and makes a space appear more fluid. These arcs are easy on the eye and restful. More tightly rounded forms or sharp angles

ABOVE **This useful kitchen counter, with its work surface and built-in sink, helps to contain the kitchen in this compact flat while also dividing the dining and cooking areas.**

create greater visual tension. They are more emphatic and can be very effective in screening small areas, such as an entrance. It is possible to play tricks on the eye by marking out areas in irregular shapes. A triangular or circular space, or an irregular rectangle can be visually exciting and create an impression of a larger space.

Dividing walls that lean are exciting too – gently inclined inwards they feel protective, while leaning outwards they are liberating.

LEFT  A curved wall gently embraces this sunny dining area and lightflow continues into the centre of the house. The shape of the wall is echoed in the ceiling-recessed lights which edge an oval cut-out.

BELOW  A handsome multi-purpose divider that separates two spaces, provides masses of storage and display space and is a richly coloured monolith.

The room divider has become an incredibly useful tool in the interior designer's bag of tricks. Made of wood or laminated panels, dividers can be solid, grand and monumental – solidly standing their ground between rooms and providing a tremendous amount of storage and display space. At the other end of the spectrum they can be elegant and light structures of glass, perspex or steel that just hint at separation.

# sliding and oversize doors

Flexible alternatives to walls include screens on wheels, sliding partitions, and hanging screens. Even the lightest suggestion of a division – a Japanese-style screen – can define an area without the need for full-scale floor-to-ceiling walls. Light can flow freely and the eye is drawn through the space.

The sliding screen/door has undergone a recent renaissance. This means of closing off spaces last enjoyed a heyday in the 1960s and 1970s when it appeared in millions of modern homes. However, the technology was never quite fully

BELOW The style of this apartment is one of simplicity and minimalism. The complex shapes and finishes of the kitchen can be hidden by sliding a glass panel across the opening.

developed – the nylon tracks and wheels were often flimsy and countless sliding doors careered right out of favour to be replaced with doors on hinges. But with the much-improved track systems, strong enough to take weighty glass and steel panels, the sliding wall/door is

back. The mechanism is not only wonderfully theatrical, it is also incredibly space-efficient.

At the same time as engineers were improving tracks, work was underway improving pivots for hanging very heavy doors. Using these systems fitted to floor and ceiling, vast doors the size of walls can be swung open and shut with no more effort than it takes to move a traditional door hung on side hinges. These large panels look particularly impressive if made from the same materials as the adjoining walls. Once again the sense of drama is hugely appealing.

ABOVE A wall that becomes a door. This really magnificent wood panel swings open for access, but when closed resumes its role as part of the wall.

# glazed screens

In defining space, the glazed screen offers the best of both worlds; it is practical and decorative. The screen acts as powerful visual punctuation and offers high degrees of transparency and lightflow.

In deciding how to divide living space, it is important to consider the effect you are trying to achieve. Glazing can be elegant and cool, but if you need a really substantial barrier, it may be more appropriate to choose a solid material.

Frames for screens can be constructed in a range of materials, most commonly timber or steel, and are available in ready-made systems. If your budget is generous you might prefer something tailor-made to echo architectural details such as the pattern of window panes or door panelling. There is also the possibility of commissioning an artist to make up individual panels or an entire screen.

There are plenty of options in the types of glazing too – clear, opaque, coloured, or decorated with sandblasting or acid-etching. For obvious safety reasons, toughened glass must be used in the home. Your supplier will offer advice on the types of glass to be used and the recommended thicknesses.

Once again, the design possibilities are endless; screens can be minimal planes suspended in space that merely hint at separation, they can be colourful panels of irregular shape that make a powerful visual statement, or they can form entire translucent walls.

LEFT This lacy effect of this glass and metal panel makes a really subtle, but necessary, division between the home office/study and the living area.

BELOW This three-quarter-height screen, with opaque glass, defines the kitchen and the living area. The generous-sized panels echo the proportions and the pattern of the large exterior windows reflected in their surface, and the theme is picked up again at the far side of the kitchen.

# mezzanines

With the loft-living craze of the 1990s, the mezzanine has enjoyed a revival. In converting and making the most of cavernous industrial buildings, clever architects and designers looked skyward for inspiration and began inserting sleeping platforms, small work spaces, mini gymnasiums and libraries into the tops of the tall rooms. The device is simple and effective, it creates additional floor space, and adds visual interest. It also has an important effect on the space below, by making it more intimate and enclosed. The classic use of the mezzanine is as an insert into the back of a double-height living space: the additional floor makes a sleeping platform and below is a kitchen.

Of course, that formula is not rigid and can be reinterpreted for different spaces, but a generous room height of at least 4 metres (13 feet) is advisable as a starting point. This sort of height can be difficult to find in post-war housing, but along with redundant warehouses and factories, nineteenth-century houses and upmarket mansion blocks often have very high ceilings.

The mezzanine doesn't have to be large to be useful, even small spaces, providing enough room for a tiny

BELOW **In large nineteenth-century homes, room heights were generous and today provide us with the opportunity of slotting in a mezzanine-level bedroom.**

office, can be a real bonus and add value to a property. While the simplest solution is to insert a rectangular platform, it is also worth considering the use of different shapes like the L-shape, that wraps around the entire room. Whichever you choose, care should be taken to ensure that the amount of floor space taken up by the access stairs or ladder does not cancel out the space gained. The new level should also be structurally sound and provided with a safety rail or wall.

To reduce its visual impact on a room, the mezzanine design should be kept as simple as possible and painted in the same colour, or lighter, than the rest of the room.

ABOVE **A high ceiling in a hallway can be reduced over the cloakroom and cupboard space to create a cabin-like bed platform, ideal as guest accommodation.**

# changing levels

ABOVE  While we all understand the appeal of landscaping in our gardens and the use of varied heights to add interest, we often forget that the same principles can be applied to the interior space. Here the kitchen and sitting room step down to the dining room marking it off as a special area.

When it comes to gardening we all understand how landscaping can add interest and emphasis. Creating different levels over an area of outdoor space can allow for a flower bed or perhaps a sunny spot for a garden bench. This notion has been slow to transfer to inside the home.

The use of changing levels can be a delight in an interior, because they provide a shift in tone. The means can be incredibly subtle, just one step will achieve a sense that you are entering a different realm. We know from experience that steps up lead to a stage or a viewing platform and that walking downwards takes us to basement clubs, low-ceiling wine cellars, sunken baths.

Should you decide to incorporate some interior landscaping, it's important to make sure the platform is solidly built – it has to be substantial enough to take furniture and a number of people. The height of the step is also important – too shallow and people may miss it and trip, too deep and it becomes a real effort to move around the home. A depth of between 120 and 150 millimetres (4¾-6 inches) is the most comfortable.

This landscaping device is best used sparingly, as a home filled with changing levels between every room will try your patience and simply become annoying. For maximum impact restrict yourself to just one or two changed levels and reserve them for something special – raising a dining platform, or perhaps sinking a soft seating area.

RIGHT **The sunken bath is considered the height of luxury; here a sunken effect is achieved by building a platform around the bath and steps leading up to it. By lavishing such attention on the bath, the designer has produced a celebration of bathing.**

# defining space with materials

The materials chosen to finish a room can be used not just to set a mood, but also to help us understand or 'read' the layout. Using the same materials throughout a living area will give a sense of unity and bring the whole together; however, by adding a contrast you will immediately create a separate space. This can be achieved in a number of ways – insetting panels of stone or cork in the floor, or using a different colour for the main flooring will instantly produce a change. Similarly, a large

ABOVE **Because we are highly visually literate, our eyes and brains can immediately 'read' the designer's intentions in creating these rooms. The change of flooring denotes a move into a different style of room.**

One of the most subtle, yet effective, ways of delineating space is through use of materials and colours to finish an area. Flooring is an excellent starting point and a number of inventive examples can be found in shops and hotels where flooring materials are deployed as a way of guiding people through the space. In a shop, for example, hard flooring areas in stone or concrete mark out the high-traffic circulation routes while soft areas, created with carpet or timber, surround the merchandise displays and encourage shoppers to linger.

rug surrounded by sofas will clearly signify a seating area. If you prefer to mark spaces with greater subtlety, wooden floorboards can simply be lain in a different direction from the main floor.

The same set of principles applies to walls and ceilings: by using materials of the same colour and texture you can streamline the interior and draw a space together, but any changes will be read by the eye as a break in that continuity.

The materials you choose to finish and enclose spaces with will have a huge impact on the final room and its ambience. If you need a sound barrier the walls will need to be fairly solid. However, transparency or translucency is still an option – glass bricks are effective at blocking sounds and allowing light through. Solid walls can be finished in a variety of ways and need not be restricted to the ubiquitous coat of plaster followed by paint. Other options include different styles of panelling, suede,

sheet steel, plain brick or simple timber floorboards.

Remember that lines not only delineate space but are also able to give it character. A room with predominantly horizontal lines gives the appearance of a wider, flatter, calm space, while vertical lines add energy and height; they encourage the eye to look upwards. Similarly, if floorboards are laid lengthways they create the optical illusion of elongating the space. Laid across the width of a room they will broaden it.

LEFT **The pattern of the flooring here makes a very clear statement about where one room ends and another begins, and adds pattern to generate subtle visual interest.**

ABOVE **While this living space is linked by the use of the same timber flooring throughout, the spaces are defined with colour – the pink marks out the kitchen and, in the distance, green signals an informal eating area with wonderful views.**

# defining space with light

The quality of a space can be improved immeasurably with good lighting. Le Corbusier defined architecture as 'sculpture seen under light'. He saw that it is possible to change the perception of a room by allowing in more natural light and by improving artificial lighting schemes.

There are few things more gloomy and uninspiring than a room lit by a single, central pendant light, but the very same space can be taken into another realm if illuminated with lights of different types and at different heights. Clever use of lighting can create the effect you want, whether it's warm and intimate or cool and fresh.

Getting lighting just right is a skill and, unless you are a natural, it will take some experimenting. Take a look around you at the lighting in shops, restaurants, theatres and other people's homes. Try and work out what makes the schemes successful. Lighting in shops, for example, has become an art form. The smartest shops have complex lighting programmes which alter throughout

BELOW Light is one of the most subtle and effectives means we have of defining and altering the character of space. Here crisp and twinkly halogen lights mark out the kitchen work area. Uplighting above the units gives a warm wash to the lowered ceiling at the back of the kitchen.

the day – the night-time sequence, when the store is closed, might focus attention on the window displays; while for daytime it creates a sense of depth in the shop and so draws its customers further inside.

Good lighting design is determined by a number of factors: the size, height and style of the room; its uses; the direction of natural light; the types of lamp you wish to use; and the quality of the light – robust Mediterranean light, for example, is very different from the cooler tones of Scandinavia.

Take careful stock of your rooms: a living room in the northern hemisphere that faces west should have a good supply of natural light throughout most of the year. In the same house, an east-facing kitchen will need good task lighting because it will be darker in the evenings while dinner is being cooked.

The height of the room will also affect what you do with lighting; you can choose to exaggerate its height using powerful uplighters that wash the walls to the junction with the ceiling, or you can make the space more intimate by artificially lowering the ceiling using low-level lighting and lamps no higher than the dado rail or at average ceiling height.

Of course the mood you want to create is vital to informing the scheme you design. It is quite likely that you will want different types of light at different times (a family supper will generally be more brightly lit than a formal supper with friends), so build in flexibility. You may want to highlight a sculpture, a display of flowers or an architectural detail to add drama, or create the unexpected by setting lights into floors or into walls at the skirting level (this works particularly well in stairs and hallways).

You may also want to use light to mark out entire areas, a track of spotlights above a freestanding kitchen counter or island unit will cast a curtain of light that divides a room.

Different lights are designed for particular functions. As the name suggests, an uplighter throws light upwards to reflect off the walls and ceiling to provide a soft indirect light for a space. This effect can be achieved through wall-mounted lights or freestanding units such as tall uplighter lamps. In both cases the majority of light is prevented from falling downwards as the light bulb is set in an opaque holder.

Downlighting can be used for adding a wash of illumination or as a directional beam (through ceiling-recessed and pendant light fittings, and in tracks holding several light fittings). Some of the most beautiful downlighting effects are achieved with low-voltage halogen lamps, which have a sparkling crystal quality. Tracks of lights can cast washes of light down walls, while single lamps can create dramatic pools of light on floors or the object they are pointed at. Halogen lamps are available in a variety of voltages and in designs to cast different beam widths.

Spotlights provide the means to highlight an area or object using a narrow and often intense beam of light. Different effects can be achieved depending on the positioning and direction of the light.

# space studies

## sources of inspiration

The sheer ingenuity of the architect in reshaping houses and apartments has to be seen to be believed. Even the most unpromising-looking places can be transformed into really desirable homes. And there's no better source of inspiration for your own project than taking a look at others. Some ideas shown in the following pages can be simply recycled wholesale, others will need to be adapted to suit your particular property.

The projects appear in three sections called *adding space*, *reinventing space* and *making space*. The first includes a variety of clever ideas for breaking through the boundaries of your existing space by adding extensions such as a sunny glazed pavilion, a shower cubicle or even a modest but beautifully detailed balcony. *Reinventing space* explores the ways in which we can reorder and reorganize our homes to make the best use of existing space and so tailor our rooms to truly suit our needs. It looks at a number of space-enhancing features including pierced walls and mezzanines. The final section, *making space*, delves into those underused and dead areas of the home and breathes new life into them. It demonstrates how attics, cellars and neglected areas beneath and above the stairs can be transformed into hard-working additional space. All of the projects have been carefully chosen to suit a range of budgets and tastes. They provide a wealth of ideas and inspiration and show you how to improve the quality and value of your living space.

LEFT AND ABOVE  The modern architect can create living space in the most awkward of areas. This striking kitchen has been fitted in a first floor area where there is little room for a table. However, a delightful egg-shaped glass table has been included that hovers ingeniously over the top of the stairwell. The inclined walls on the right help the space open out to receive the natural light from above.

# adding space

BELOW This timber-framed extension includes a large horseshoe-shaped area of built-in seating. This makes comfortable and precious space for resting or reading.

# kitchen/terrace extension

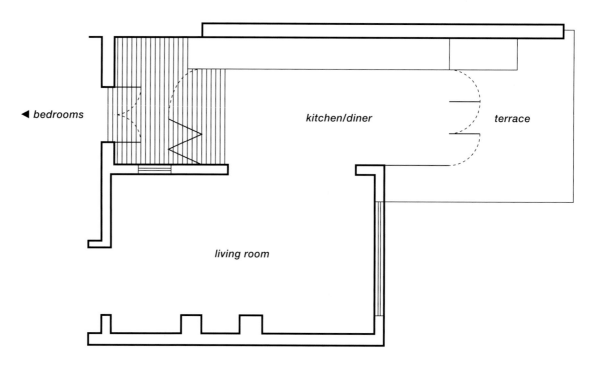

bedrooms ◄

kitchen/diner

terrace

living room

ABOVE **The plan shows clearly how the dining, cooking and exterior terrace spaces relate to one another. The tiny decked courtyard in the top left-hand corner of the plan provides a safe play area for the children and a link between their bedroom and the kitchen.**

RIGHT **The most impressive design features include the concertina doors, which fold right back to unite the inside of the apartment with the outdoors. The sense of continuous space is heightened by the long kitchen countertop made of creamy terrazzo, which extends into the garden to form a barbecue area.**

This apartment was originally part of a 1970s house conversion, which was claustrophobic and riddled with corridors. Radical changes were needed to make sense of the space. Spun around a full 180 degrees, the bedrooms have been shunted from the back of the apartment to the front, and the living and kitchen areas switched from the front to the back. The corridors have been consigned to history. The result is an open garden apartment. And right where you would expect the standard conservatory, there is a stunning, light-flooded kitchen/dining pavilion and terrace.

The replanning of this apartment is inspired but most noteworthy is the new kitchen and dining area, which has transformed an ordinary space into an incredibly exciting one.

The neat, flat-topped extension links beautifully with the repositioned living area – internal walls have almost disappeared and the whole space is tied together with limestone flooring throughout. This even stretches into the garden to create a raised terrace. The rectangular stone floortiles are laid lengthways to help 'lead' you through the space. Everywhere the eye is drawn to the outside. There are huge

## ADDING SPACE

**The brief:** Reorganize a conversion apartment to make better use of the internal space.

**The solution:** Reorient the entire apartment, moving bedrooms to the front and living areas to the back, overlooking the south-facing garden.

ABOVE Unbelievably, this space was once a windowless bathroom, a bedroom and passageway. The kitchen now stands in the new extension and, with the side wall of the house removed, an exhilarating, light-filled space has been created. Limestone flooring throughout the apartment unites it visually.

**ADDING SPACE**

new windows in the living room and glazed, made-to-measure, douglas fir doors around two sides of the end of the kitchen extension that fold away out of sight. One of the most striking features, which also carries you right outside, is the amazing 8-metre- (26-foot-) long, cream-coloured, terrazzo kitchen countertop. This runs the entire length of the kitchen and then stretches out across the terrace to form a barbecue area.

Numerous excellent design details complete the transformation. A long, slim, glass panel set into the flat roof above the countertop draws yet more natural light into the kitchen. Instead of

wall cupboards, which would have appeared too intrusive visually, there are lovely, thick glass shelves above the countertop. Cantilevered from a steel channel embedded into the wall, they provide both storage and display space. At the heart of the apartment, situated between the kitchen and the children's bedroom, there is a small, timber-decked courtyard, which not only brings light into the bedroom but also offers a safe play area. A low-level window in the living room affords views out on to the deck.

Not surprisingly, the thirty-something couple whose home this is have become keen gardeners.

LEFT  Who could resist sitting out on this sun deck? The table is drawn through the concertina doors, and it is sheltered enough to eat outside for much of the year.

BELOW  The long countertop and limestone flooring draw the eye outside where the garden provides a calming and restful backdrop to the living space.

# pivoting glass wall

ABOVE  This extension had been a scruffy, single-storey affair looking out on to a dismal back yard. By rebuilding it and adding another floor, the house now has an upstairs office and a new dining area.

RIGHT  The pivoting wall is based on the principle of a garage door. It swings a full 90 degrees from a vertical to a horizontal position, cleverly transforming itself from an exterior wall to a sheltering canopy.

**The brief:** Create space for entertaining in a small house and transform the dismal back yard.

**The solution:** Rebuild the existing extension. Incorporate a whole wall of glass that flips up to open the house on to the back yard, and makes the perfect space for parties.

Although she loved her terrace house, the flamboyant owner, who works in the fashion business, did not have enough space to hold dinner parties – the small rooms simply weren't big enough to accommodate a large table. In addition, she wanted to make better use of a small and unloved back yard. Fortunately, her architect came up with the perfect solution straight away.

A previous ramshackle, single-storey extension, which was poorly built and contributed little to the house in looks or usefulness, has been replaced by a two-storey structure on the same site. The upstairs is now a study, filled with natural light that is drawn in through large skylights set at a raked angle in the flat roof. Downstairs, the dining area, which extends still further into the courtyard, has a long slice of glazing set into its roof. But, most exciting of all is the ingenious, pivoting glass wall. Imitating the movement of a garage door, this wall swings upwards and outwards into the courtyard where it can be locked horizontally to make a covered, light-filled dining and party area.

Using glass in this way has succeeded in breaking down the barriers between indoors and out. A seamless space has been created that retains a connection with the outdoors and is sheltered enough to make eating al fresco possible in virtually all weathers.

The great pivoting slab of glass, which is made up of four rectangular panels of glass, is held in a steel

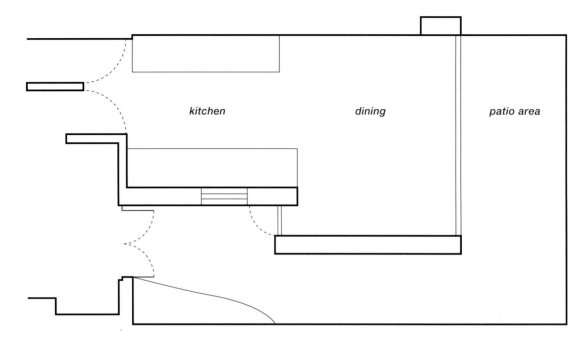

| kitchen | dining | patio area |

ABOVE  In this Victorian terrace house, with its typically small rooms, the pivoting glass wall allows the dining area to extend into the courtyard and double its size.

RIGHT  With the courtyard very much a part of the new living space, the owner has developed a keen interest in gardening. By painting the dining room walls and the exterior brick walls white, a sense of continuity has been created and light is reflected back into the house.

frame. Built by a local metalworker more accustomed to producing garden gates, the frame is double-glazed with toughened and laminated glass weighing a massive ¾ tonne. This is counterbalanced with lead weights and the whole movement is electronically controlled. A neat clip ensures the 'wall' is held in its horizontal position, although the engineering of the mechanism is so precise it really isn't required.

The once-neglected courtyard has now become an integral part of the living space. The walls are painted white to match the colour scheme in the house and to help reflect light back inside. The owner has now discovered that she has green fingers and has started to decorate the area with terracotta pots filled with greenery and unusual stone statues.

# ADDING SPACE

# small balcony

ABOVE Small can be beautiful. This tiny balcony is exquisitely detailed with its slatted wood benching and decking and built-in zinc planters. In contrast to the horizontal lines of bricks and slats, the jaunty vertical railing design adds a visual lift and leads the eye to the gardens and sky beyond.

## ADDING SPACE

To make additional outdoor space in a first-floor apartment that is part of a house conversion can be difficult. In this case, the move to build an elegant balcony was hastened when the neighbours downstairs announced they wanted to extend their conservatory.

The new structure had to be large enough to provide room for relaxing, reading and enjoying a glass of wine, but not so big that it would overshadow the new building downstairs. The solution was this simple balcony that rests on a slender part of the roof of the conservatory below. It has a curved prow, which gives around 1 metre (3 foot) of floorspace, but which swells out to 1.5 metre (5 foot) at its deepest point to accommodate the slatted wooden bench.

A zinc-lined planter for flowers at either end of the bench is a thoughtful touch. To emphasize the effect of opening out the space, new French doors, replacing the windows, link the living space with the balcony.

The brief: Create an outdoor area in which to relax on warm evenings.

The solution: Add a balcony off the bedroom that will span the two exterior walls and is cantilevered out over the conservatory below. Replace the existing glass with French windows.

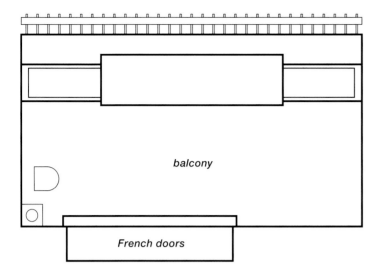

balcony

French doors

LEFT  It was impossible to build the balcony out very far because of the glazed conservatory below. However, by curving the balcony like the prow of a ship, the seating extends beyond the floor area.

BELOW  Although small, the balcony does add to the quality of the interior space. The open French doors allow in extra light and make the bedroom feel much larger.

# shower cubicle

Older family homes that have just one bathroom simply don't provide enough washing facilities for the average modern household. In this modest house, the solution to the morning and evening washtime rush-hour was to push out sideways through the wall of the downstairs lavatory and build on a cylindrical pod containing a beautiful, generous-sized shower. As the owner was working to a limited budget, the architect kept the new addition as compact as possible and building costs to a minimum.

The shower is set in a neat, three-quarters-enclosed drum alongside the hand basin and the toilet. There is no need for a shower curtain as the drum contains the water when the shower is on, keeping the area around the basin and toilet as dry as possible.

ABOVE In this lean-to with a difference, the shower cubicle breaks out through the corner of the building to make an interesting sculptural shape in the garden.

RIGHT The smooth, curved surface of the exterior is continued inside the lean-to where the shower cubicle joins what was originally the outside wall.

**ADDING SPACE**

The brief: Improve the small downstairs lavatory and add a shower.

The solution: Remove the corner of the lean-to and replace it with a shower pod, and extend the lavatory to make a very useful washing area.

And there's no shower tray either – the floor of the shower is also the floor of the washroom. Water drains away through a hole inset directly into the floor in the centre of the pod.

The walls and floors are finished in the simplest of materials: rough-and-ready concrete render that has been covered with several coats of hardwearing waterproof paint in sunshine yellow. The exterior of the lean-to, meanwhile, has been painted a rich terracotta red. As well as complementing the plant pots, the terracotta emphasizes the striking sculptural quality of the lean-to.

The shower is great fun to use and the ideal place to cool off after a few hours of gardening on a hot day.

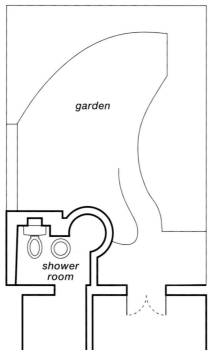

*garden*

*shower room*

ABOVE  In this simple and practical room, the stainless-steel fittings add real sparkle. The circular form of the shower is echoed in the hand basin.

LEFT  The shape of the shower is extremely economical and efficient with space but it is also intriguing, introducing a lovely rotund shape to the garden.

# reinventing space

BELOW LEFT Even small interventions can transform a space. Open stairs, minimal balustrading and French windows help to create a light, fresh-feeling room.

BELOW RIGHT The simplest ideas are often the most effective. A corridor is reinterpreted by marking the circulation route with a tall and substantial freestanding bookcase.

# open-plan living and dining

This modern extension was designed for the new owners of a turn-of-the-century house. They wanted an informal, family living space adjoining the more formal house.

With two daughters approaching their teens, the owners had a very specific brief. There had to be a place where the adults could enjoy peace and quiet, but also space in which the children could be noisy. In addition, they needed a living area where everyone could get together to eat and watch television.

Accommodating such varied and even conflicting needs was a tough challenge, but the architect's solution has pleased everyone. The result is a dual-personality home.

Because the older part of the house is of historic interest, remodelling it was out of the question. Instead, it has been sympathetically restored. This now provides sleeping accommodation for the adults and a formal living room and study. Meanwhile, the single-storey extension has been replaced with a contemporary-style, two-storey structure. Upstairs, there is a bathroom and two bedrooms for the children, along with their own small study and television room. The area is acoustically separate from the main house, which means the children can play loud music without disturbing their parents. Linked

**REINVENTING SPACE**

**The brief:** Create a new family space catering for growing children and adults.

**The solution:** A modern, informal, open-plan extension adjoining the older traditional house, with the upper level given over solely to the children.

ABOVE  The flame-orange sofa sets the tone
of this modern, light-filled extension. This
part of the extension is the communal living
area where the whole family can dine
together and watch the television.

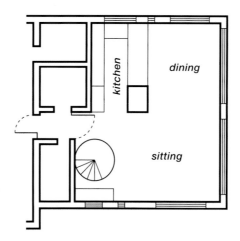

kitchen

dining

sitting

RIGHT **The Edwardian main house and the new extension are separate entities with different characters and different functions.**

BELOW **The slit windows draw in light as the sun travels around the house. The custom-made television and music unit can be moved around the room as desired.**

by a spiral staircase, the ground-level space is open-plan, containing a kitchen and dining and seating areas.

Finishes are simple, low-cost and durable. The walls are painted a plain off-white and, except for the tiled kitchen area, the floor is covered with a rich aubergine-coloured carpet. The feel of the extension is deliberately different from the main part of the house, and designed to reflect modern family needs. Even the style of the

# REINVENTING SPACE

furnishings is a contrast – in the Edwardian house the furniture is of the appropriate period, while a flame-orange, contemporary sofa sets the tone in the extension.

Inspired details include the architect's handling of light. The house is surrounded by high walls and other buildings, and so to draw in as much natural light as possible, a sequence of long vertical and horizontal slit windows slash through every wall of the extension. These high- and low-level slits take their turn at catching the light as the sun moves around the

house. The play of light animates the space and changes the atmosphere at different times of the day. Even at the very end of the day, light cascades down the stairs through a carefully positioned rooflight.

Artworks have been given their own display cases. Small sculptures, collected by the couple have been recessed into the walls and then top-lit. The architect also designed much of the furniture, including the television and music unit which is on castors so that it can be moved easily around the room.

ABOVE **The kitchen is built into a corner of the extension. A wall recess at the entrance to the kitchen makes an intriguing display case for the sculpture.**

# bedroom/dressing room

**REINVENTING SPACE**

**ABOVE** Crisp, white bed linen, white-painted wood and the clear coastal light streaming in through the windows combine to give this room a tremendous sense of calm and tranquillity. The very simple headboard forms the back of a clever storage system, which also screens off the dressing area.

The owners of this modest house on the coast fell in love with the sea views and beach walks, but felt their home was not quite in harmony with its beautiful surroundings. Built of brick and organized into a series of smallish rooms, it felt rather ordinary. The architect at once saw an opportunity to borrow from the style of the classic beach hut. She lined the internal walls

**The brief:** Relate a seaside home more closely to its location.

**The solution:** Use natural wood and pale colours to create the feeling of a beach hut. Remove the bedroom ceiling and build in a freestanding unit to provide storage space.

with boarding and laid the floor with oak, which had been treated with chlorine, to give it the lovely silver-grey colour of driftwood. Colours through the house are pale blues and creams.

The main bedroom is large, but the low ceiling gave the space a slightly oppressive quality. By removing the ceiling and opening the space up to the rafters, the room feels entirely different – uplifting and charged with energy. As well as making this simple but radical change, the bed has been pulled into the centre of the

room and its headboard doubles as a freestanding cupboard with shelves. It even incorporates a small office area complete with a fax machine. This can be closed up when not in use.

The headboard/cupboard also acts as a screen to make a small dressing area behind the bed. Here, a run of floor-to-ceiling wardrobes has been built along the length of the back wall.

To give the room an additional lift, there are discreet uplighters fitted into the top of the wardrobes, throwing light up to the rafters.

BELOW **The headboard/cupboard is used for storing clothes in drawers, but also contains a fax machine and worktop, which can be closed up, as shown, when not in use.**

# glass-roofed kitchen

Working with buildings of historical interest is a sensitive business; the balance has to be struck between preserving the past and making a liveable home in the present. In this project, decades of shambolic, piecemeal extensions to an early nineteenth-century, two-storey cottage were dramatically reinvented as a streamlined interior with an elegant, glass-roofed kitchen.

The owner of the cottage originally called in the architects to redesign his bathroom. However, once discussions were under way, he became so enthused with the project that he asked them to take on the remodelling of the entire cottage.

The most remarkable part of the project was the makeover of the ground floor. Previous owners had already removed the wall between the two adjacent ground-floor rooms and so the space was already brighter than in neighbouring houses, but the old extensions were badly built and gloomy. The architect kept the shell of the largest extension, now the dining room, and then slotted in the glass structure between this and the house

**RIGHT** Extensions and lean-tos had been added to this cottage over the years in an *ad hoc* way. Once the accretion became an annoying jumble, it had to be rationalized.

**CENTRE** Previous owners of this house had already carried out work remodelling the interior. The new work concentrated on bringing order to the kitchen area.

**FAR RIGHT** The new-look extension is a superb solution to the earlier mishmash. The glazed roof draws in lots of extra light and the long countertop running right into the garden connects the indoor and outdoor spaces.

## REINVENTING SPACE

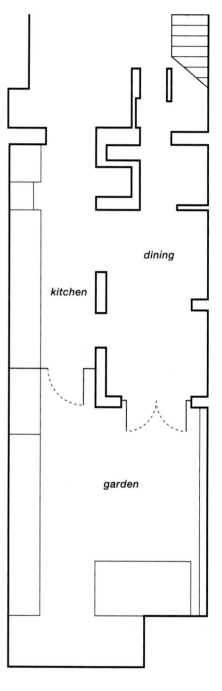

**The brief:** Transform the lean-to into a streamlined, light-filled kitchen.

**The solution:** Dismantle the old extension and replace it with a simple glazed box to contain the kitchen, which runs the length of the party wall.

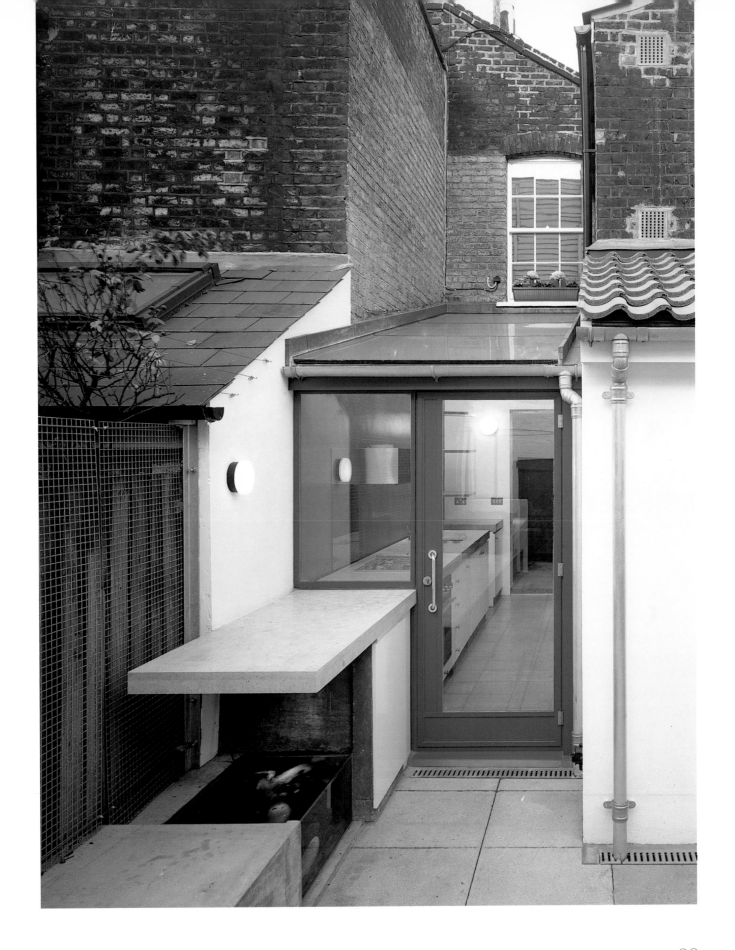

next door. The kitchen units, ranged below the countertop, were kept to a minimum to give a greater sense of space. As much light as possible was drawn into the dining area by replacing a window in the main extension with French windows and fitting a glass door and roof to the new kitchen.

Powerful design devices link the inside and the outside; the same concrete flooring slabs have been used for the extensions and the redesigned garden, and a long, limestone kitchen countertop extends out through the kitchen wall to form a garden counter, which floats over the fishtank beneath. When the doors are open, the ground floor and garden feel like one room and make an ideal space for parties and al fresco dining.

The success of the work is in the beautiful detailing and also in respecting the scale of the original building – larger extensions would almost certainly have overwhelmed the small cottage. Interestingly, although modern materials including concrete, glass and steel have been incorporated, they have provided the perfect foil for the original timber flooring, stairs and panelling that have now become focal points.

## REINVENTING
## SPACE

RIGHT **The long, horizontal lines of the kitchen create a feeling of calm in this space. Wall units were not used as they would have caused the room to appear smaller and cluttered. The brilliant cobalt-blue wall gives a visual lift.**

# pierced walls

BELOW **It would have been almost impossible and very expensive to remove this structural wall. Instead, it has been pierced to allow views and light into the room.**

This two-storey apartment, carved from a small, defunct, 1950s office block, is ranged over the ground and lower ground floors. The immediate challenge was to bring in as much light to the apartment as possible, while creating a series of interesting spaces.

The apartment now sits where the lift and stairs once climbed through the building. The space had to incorporate three bedrooms and a generous-sized living room. Since there were structural walls in the lower ground floor of the building that could not be removed,

**REINVENTING SPACE**

The brief: Inject as much light as possible into the living area.

The solution: Move the bedrooms to the lower floor and the living room to the upper floor.

Pierce the walls with holes to make doorways and create internal windows to frame views.

it was decided to place the bedrooms below the living area where the slightly darker spaces are better suited to sleeping. By locating the living spaces on the floor above it meant there would be as much light as possible in the living quarters.

To allow the maximum amount of light to flow through the space, the walls have been pierced with internal doorways, often without doors, and unglazed windows, which also provide glimpses through the entire floor. The openings give all the advantages of an open-plan design by creating intriguing vistas, while at the same time allowing a certain amount of privacy. In the kitchen and sitting areas, for example, the wall provides a screen between the two rooms, while open doorways make the spaces feel linked.

The stairs between the two floors of the apartment are also completely open to enhance the sense of space. Opening this meant that fire officers were consulted and regulations had to be closely adhered to as fire and smoke would spread rapidly with nothing to impede them. To help in an escape from fire, French windows leading to a garden area were added to the bedrooms.

LEFT **High-quality finishes and simple shapes are very sculptural. Internal windows make excellent frames for views and transform a bowl of fruit into a striking still-life image.**

# mezzanine

In this raised ground-floor apartment, the architect has performed a small miracle of alchemy and transformed a deeply unpromising space into one that is highly desirable.

The rooms in this early twentieth-century mansion block were blessed with high ceilings but, unfortunately, the apartment had been the victim of an extremely clumsy 1970s conversion when the mezzanine sleeping area/office was inserted. Its present owner had tried various ways of brightening up the space but had found the apartment so difficult to love that she eventually put it up for sale.

ABOVE A serene space has been sculpted from what was once an overwhelming dazzle of swirly carpets and loud, patterned wallpaper. A poorly built, makeshift mezzanine, complete with an ornate balustrade, has been swapped for this elegantly simple and contemporary one.

RIGHT The plan demonstrates a masterpiece of space organization. As the owner doesn't enjoy baths, a huge walk-in shower has been built in the small bathroom. The kitchen has been streamlined and given a large dining table, while the mezzanine floats overhead to form a home office and guest bedroom.

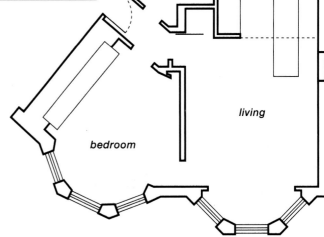

**REINVENTING
SPACE**

**The brief:** Make better use of the space and resite the intrusive stairs.

**The solution:** Strip out the apartment, pulling the mezzanine slightly forward into the room.

Reposition the stairs at the back and build in a sleek, modern kitchen.

For months and months there were no takers at the right price, so she made the decision to stay but called in professional help.

The key to the architect's solution for transforming the space was to free up the vast back wall and resite the stairs, which intruded badly into the living area. The bathroom had also eaten into the living room space so more floor area was reclaimed by dispensing with the bath, shrinking the space, and making a large shower room instead, which, incidentally, was the owner's preference.

The mezzanine was pulled a little further into the room and away from the back wall, leaving a gap. This made the wall appear sheer and quite impressive, and allowed a discreet ship's ladder to be fixed at the back of the kitchen, away from the main living space, to link the two levels. With the stairs now out of the way, there is additional room in the living space for another sofa.

The entire space was cleared of its cacophony of visual clutter and recast as a sleek, calm, clean-lined sequence of areas. The large, solid maple table is fixed in place and the oven has been fitted into its kitchen end. Stretching into the living area, the table links this to the cooking section.

RIGHT **The neat ship's ladder at the back of the kitchen gives access to the mezzanine. The desk upstairs is built over the top of the kitchen and bathroom.**

# flexible space

ABOVE **Streamlined and discreet, the pale-coloured walls in the living area are, in fact, a series of doors with a variety of functions. One leads to the bathroom, or shower room, others open to reveal a wardrobe and pull-down guest bed, while the remainder are simply cupboards.**

## REINVENTING SPACE

There are many occasions when it is simply not possible to physically enlarge your home, especially when you live in a purpose-built block of apartments. However, inspired thinking can help you use the space you do have to best effect, at the same time creating the illusion that your home is much bigger than it really is.

This small, two-bedroom apartment on the fourth floor of a 1970s block has been completely reinvented. Once a poky collection of rooms off a central corridor, it is now an extremely flexible, open and welcoming space. Originally, there were three tiny bedrooms, but it was decided to sacrifice one to enhance the quality of the whole.

**The brief:** Reconfigure a small, two-bedroom apartment to create a streamlined space with light-filled and open, versatile living areas.

**The solution:** A central cube with doors for walls.

ABOVE  The bathroom opens on to the living area, partly to give the tiny room a bit of breathing space, but also to create an unexpected vista and the ultimate luxury of being able to watch television in the bath.

RIGHT  This apartment is not much bigger than a hotel suite, and is a fine example of how to make the best use of space.

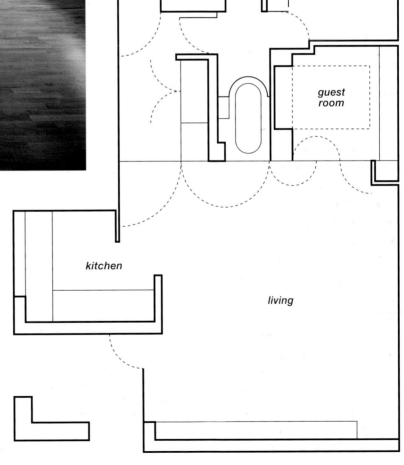

bathroom

bedroom

guest room

kitchen

living

The key to the redesign was the central 'magic box'. The architect stripped away the existing corridors and walls, and placed the bathroom at the heart of the apartment. This is linked to the now much-enlarged general living area by massive doors that slide back into the walls.

Acknowledging the importance of informal spaces in the home, the architect has used sliding doors throughout the apartment, making it possible to open up the entire area and allow light to flood in. With his intense dislike of windowless internal bathrooms, he has made every effort to reduce the possible sensation of claustrophobia. One sliding door allows access from the bedroom to make it en suite, while a second opens into the living area. However, when privacy is needed, the doors can simply be closed. The doors in effect act as disappearing walls.

The walls of the box also open to reveal an enormous, fold-up dining table, which is large enough to seat six people comfortably, and a pull-down guest bed.

The apartment is bursting with clever design details that enhance the available space. Sandblasted glass panels in both the kitchen and bathroom allow in additional light, while floor-to-ceiling cupboards provide valuable but discreet storage space. The colour scheme – white and pale mushroom – is inspired, too, helping give order to the space and enhancing the natural light.

# REINVENTING SPACE

ABOVE **An ingenious and economical use of space: the vertical towel rail keeps linen tidy, while water from the spacious shower is contained by a simple glass screen.**

RIGHT **One whole section of the magic box opens to reveal a pull-down guest bed. Wardrobe space is provided at the side and there is additional storage above.**

# en suite bathroom

As this small apartment was located close to the city centre, the owners were keen to have a relaxing retreat from the action on the street. It was clear from the outset that an en suite bathroom would be highly desirable, and the resulting bathroom 'box' is a touch of real luxury, as well as a masterpiece of mood manipulation, space planning and attention to detail.

In creating a stress-free living environment, the architect has used a limited palette of colours and materials to give the illusion of greater space, but also to generate a sense of calm. Soft and tactile materials, together with plenty of natural wood, emphasize the cocooning effect.

Fitting into the back of the bedroom, the bathroom is reached by a small step, giving the subliminal message that you are entering a different realm. The raised podium also imparts a sense of theatre. Sliding, sandblasted glass panels can be pulled across the opening to close off the space, if required.

The bathroom is a neat and beautifully lit box made for pampering and self-indulgence. The mirror, which extends to the ceiling and runs the length of the bath, increases the amount of light in the bathroom and reflects precious light back into the bedroom. The exquisite stainless-steel

**REINVENTING SPACE**

**The brief:** Introduce a touch of luxury with a tranquil, en suite bathroom.

**The solution:** Incorporate a theatrical and beautifully detailed bathroom 'box', with sliding glass doors, in to one end of the bedroom.

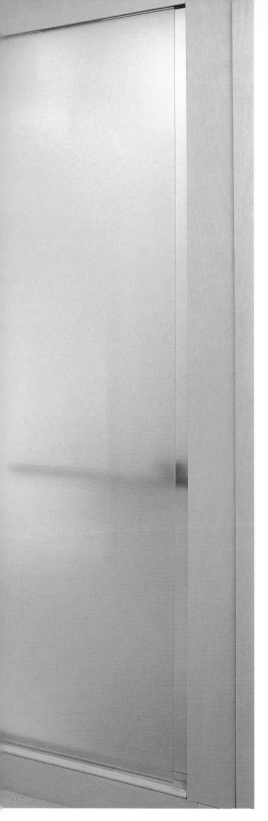

basin is set into a thick slab of glass that slots horizontally into another wall-length mirror. The glass, combined with the stainless steel and recessed ceiling lights, make the whole space appear to sparkle.

To capitalize on the high ceilings and provide extra valuable storage space, the architect has lowered the bathroom ceiling to make room for overhead cupboards, which are large enough for suitcases.

BELOW Although the contemporary bathroom fittings are simple, they provide all the luxury you would expect to find in a smart, stylish hotel.

ABOVE The en suite bathroom takes up a minimal amount of space. When the glass doors are closed, the bathroom seems to disappear altogether.

# partitioned kitchen/diner

ABOVE **When the partition door is closed, the dining area becomes more intimate. Neat detailing includes the small, built-in canteen to the left of the door, which contains cutlery.**

**REINVENTING SPACE**

After years of being divided up into a series of small bedsit apartments, this large town house has now been converted into four family apartments. The current owners discovered the end-of-terrace house when it was an uninhabited building site and immediately fell in love with the long, sunny, first-floor gallery that wraps around the corner of the house.

**The brief:** Create a kitchen/dining area that can be divided into two separate spaces.

**The solution:** Separate the two spaces with a pivoting door that folds back to become part of the wall. Unify the room with oak flooring.

The gallery, with its great views over the neighbourhood, was the natural place for a kitchen and dining area that would work equally well as a family area, and as a space for more formal dinner parties. However, measuring more than 10 metres (33 feet) in length and less than 2.5 metres (8 feet) across, the design challenge was to prevent it from feeling like a corridor.

The fitted kitchen, which makes the most economical use of the space, includes a 5-metre (16-foot) streamlined, stainless-steel countertop, and an enormous American fridge recessed into an old chimney-breast.

Standing between the kitchen and dining areas is a huge door almost 2 metres (6½ feet) wide and hung on floor and ceiling pivots. When open, the door folds back against a slim, recessed cupboard and fits flush into the wall. When closed, it divides the gallery into two, cutting out the noise and cooking smells from the kitchen and giving the dining area a more formal atmosphere. Because the door has no frame, it acts as a continuation of the wall, whether it is open or closed. A panel of 12-millimetre (½-inch) toughened glass fixed to the end of the kitchen countertop butts up to the door when it is closed so light flows between the two spaces.

LEFT **The partly opened pivoting door reveals storage shelves behind. Beyond the dining table, doors open out on to a sunny boardwalk terrace.**

BELOW **The slim, narrow space was handled confidently and inspiringly by the architect, who divided it exactly in half with the pivoting door of the storage cupboard.**

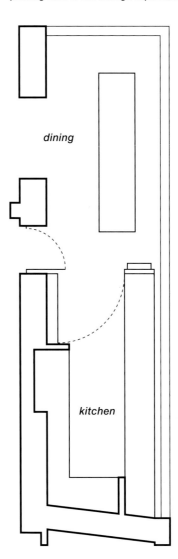

*dining*

*kitchen*

# mews conversion

Once a warren of small rooms, this seventeenth-century building had originally provided the staff quarters for a large and extremely grand town house. Set in a quiet courtyard, the structure has been put to a variety of different uses through the centuries. Most recently, the top floors have been occupied by a painter who needed plenty of natural light and an open space big enough to take very large canvases. The interior of the apartment was gutted and reshaped to make a large studio area and a sleeping space at the mezzanine level.

The entire space is open to the rafters and is painted in an off-white, making it feel deceptively large. At the lower level, the oak floor has been cleaned up and resealed to provide a pale base. The boards run lengthways through the space and draw the eye towards the windows. Also at this level there is a small, well-detailed fitted kitchen with sliding glass windows that open on to the dining area that is also under the mezzanine. This dining space is marked out with a rug and a large, simple stone-topped table.

The L-shaped mezzanine floats above to provide sleeping space and a bathroom. It is reached by a spiral staircase painted gunmetal grey. The bedroom is separated from the living area only by waist-high glass panels

**REINVENTING SPACE**

ABOVE This sleeping area is as simple as it's possible to imagine, consisting of a bed, two tables and two lamps. Possessions and clutter are stowed away in cupboards built round the walls of the flat. The glass balustrading allows natural light to flow down to the floor below.

RIGHT This atrium made by the L-shaped mezzanine is ideal painting space and can accommodate enormous canvases. The skylights allow plenty of natural light to flood in. The kitchen and dining area sit under the mezzanine with the sleeping area suspended above.

**The brief:** To create a simple space, free of visual clutter.

**The solution:** A simple box with a mezzanine, which is filled with natural light. Simple materials and storage space are provided in the large floor-to-ceiling cupboards.

# REINVENTING
# SPACE

ABOVE The simple frame for the glazed door and sliding windows of the kitchen are finished in the same gunmetal grey as the spiral stairs. The glass is an industrial type, toughened with a wire grid. Built under the mezzanine, this feels the most intimate space in the flat.

walls and ceiling. By restricting the colours and textures the architect was able to answer the very strict brief. Possessions and everyday clutter have been hidden from view by storage provided at the back of the space. Here, an entire wall is fitted with floor-to-ceiling cupboards that have sliding doors.

LEFT AND BELOW **Two central glass panels slide back to open on to the dining area and provide a serving hatch. The industrial aesthetic is continued in the kitchen, with white tiles and plain, tough finishes. The plan shows the simplicity of the layout.**

set into a minimal steel frame. The mezzanine wraps around the heart of the flat to provide an atrium lit by skylights, and here the studio space is double height.

The whole flat has been kept as simple as possible since the artist specified that visual distraction was to be kept to an absolute minimum. The palette of materials is limited to just glass, steel, oak and white-painted

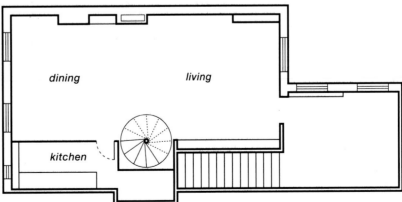

# making space

BELOW LEFT Architects are optimists and will always find ways of squeezing the most out of a space. Every corner, cupboard and pocket of space presents an opportunity.

BELOW RIGHT With a little imagination, extra sleeping space can be created anywhere. This tent-like area in the rafters might not be ideal for regular use but is great for a guest.

# kitchen under stairs

This must be a strong candidate for the ultimate in minimal kitchens. There are plenty of homes where space is at a premium and where the owners are not interested in preparing vast and complex meals. In such cases, a tiny kitchen is a great space saver. This extremely clever design borrows from the experience gained in fitting kitchens into boats and caravans. It is streamlined and does manage to accommodate a fully working kitchen. Within this tiny triangle of space there is a sink and electric hob as well as a microwave oven. The storage capacity is deceptively good with shelving above the surface, two very large drawers below the hob, cupboards and, most inventive of all, a row of deep drawers at floor level. This space, where the feet of the units sit on the floor, is usually unused, but the construction here allows this entire base to be transformed into deep, capacious storage drawers. The single spotlight lifts the corner area of the space and the pale grey and off-white finishes help to reduce the kitchen's visual impact, making it disappear into the side of this narrow room.

In addition to tailoring the kitchen to fit an awkward space, the architect has also created a small dining area which is able to seat up to four.

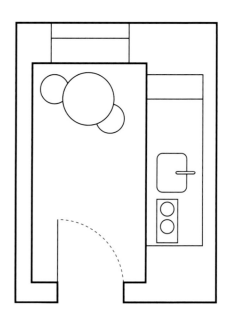

RIGHT The available space was clearly limited, but the architect has not only managed to fit in a kitchen but has also found space for a small table and chairs.

BELOW This awkward space is now able to accommodate an attractive dining area. By placing it near the window, the architect is able to make full use of the natural light.

**MAKING SPACE**

**The brief:** To make a compact and streamlined kitchen.

**The solution:** A triangle of fitted cupboards and shelving under the stairs to make a fully functioning kitchen.

ABOVE An excellent use of this compact space, making a minimal but efficient kitchen. The kickboard below the cupboard doors is usually a dead area, but not here where it becomes a series of drawers.

# cellar conversion

There was no place to go but down into the cellar to make this elegant, contemporary bathroom.

In the early 1950s, this large Victorian villa was divided into apartments. The conversion was rough-and-ready, and in the basement apartment one of the largest rooms was simply chopped in two to form a kitchen and bathroom. The present owners wanted to turn the room back into one space and make a large kitchen/dining area, but they had no idea where to resite the bathroom.

The architect came up with the answer: the disused and slightly damp coal store. The problem of the low ceiling was resolved by excavating a further 90 centimetres (3 feet) below ground, a substantial task that necessitated underpinning the entire house. A concrete floor paved with limestone replaces the original dirt floor, and the new damp-proofing has done away with any musty smells. The narrow, dark space has been transformed into a long, slender and elegant bathroom.

**MAKING SPACE**

RIGHT  The subtle lighting scheme gives this bathroom a classy finish. All the materials used have been chosen with great care; the cream limestone is particularly successful.

**The brief:** To turn a damp, disused coal store into a chic bathroom.

**The solution:** Heighten the space and finish off the conversion with limestone flooring, mosaic tiles and discreet, atmospheric lighting.

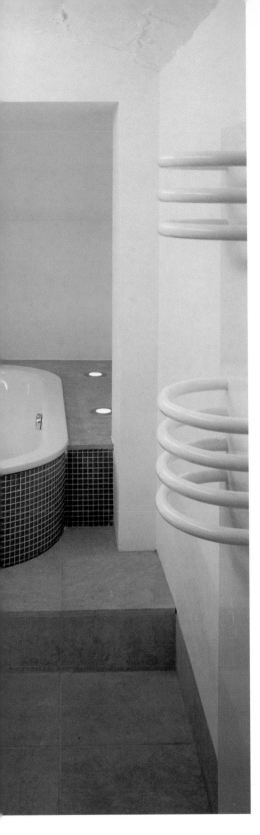

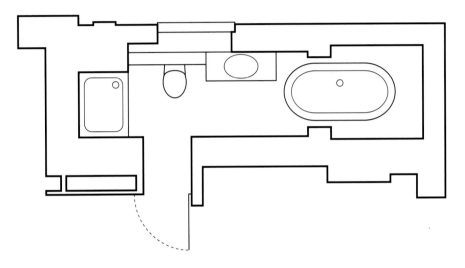

Nice touches include the long slit of a window in the wall just above ground level. This lets in just a glimmer of light but provides the eye with relief from solid walls and cleverly saves the room from feeling like a bunker.

To keep everything as simple and streamlined as possible, the palette of materials has been severely limited, although it does include limestone on the floor and countertops. Discreet lighting has been fitted into the top and bottom of the walls to provide a subtle glow and reduce visual intrusion by keeping the fittings out of sight.

ABOVE Although space was very limited, the architect has made a feature of the unusual double-round end bath and has even found room to incorporate a large shower.

# attic conversion

ABOVE This bedroom is a peaceful retreat when children and family life become overwhelming. The headboard doubles as a room divider and provides storage space.

RIGHT This was a typical attic – gloomy, neglected and stacked high with family junk. The architect saw immediately that it was the ideal space for an extra bedroom.

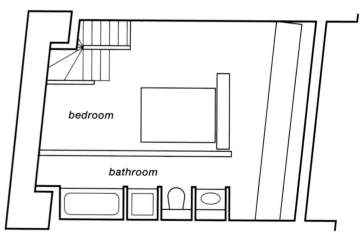

bedroom

bathroom

## MAKING SPACE

The brief: To make a quiet haven for the owners who have a growing family.

The solution: To add twin dormer windows to the rear of the house and create a light-filled bedroom with its own fully fitted en suite bathroom.

The owners of this house have a growing family, and when they realized that they needed an extra bedroom, they had to choose between creating space for it somewhere in their house, or moving. The family were very happy in their neighbourhood and their house, and so the architect seized the opportunity of reclaiming and transforming the dark, cluttered and unused attic.

The initial idea was to open up the roof to make an additional bedroom for the parents, with an en suite bathroom and a sunny roof terrace. However, local conservation laws curtailed such daring plans. The local authority wanted to retain the basic roof shape and so the roof terrace idea had to be abandoned. Instead the modified, approved plan allowed just the addition of two dormer windows and a central glazed skylight.

Despite this slightly less ambitious scheme, a beautifully finished gem of a space has been created. And because it occupies a whole floor, it acts as a private haven for the grown-ups, away from the demands of family life.

The space is unified by a new solid maple floor, upon which sits the bed with its freestanding headboard in natural pale wood. This doubles as a room divider with built-in lighting and

BELOW **Although a very narrow space, the roof area contains a bathroom, complete with large bath and shower. It is also blessed with plenty of natural light.**

ABOVE **It is almost impossible to imagine this space was once dark and dreary. The huge skylight opens for natural ventilation while the blind cuts out unwanted light.**

RIGHT **Neat detailing includes a glass panel at the top of the stairs to allow light to fall through to the floor below. The banister echoes the angle of the roof.**

# MAKING SPACE

shelf space for a couple of books on one side and clothes storage on the back. Against the wall behind the unit, there is a series of floor-to-ceiling wardrobes. Flush doors make the wardrobes seem to disappear back into the wall.

The combination of pale colours, streamlined structure and generous natural light produces a sense of great calm and tranquility in the room. In warm weather, the glass panel in the electronically operated skylight can be opened, turning the whole bedroom

into a small terrace and giving great views of the city skyline.

An added bonus of reclaiming the roof space is the creation of a streamlined, linear bathroom. Finished in just three materials – limestone, stainless steel and glass – it is filled with light from one of the new dormer windows. The matching window is positioned over the stairwell and lights the stairs and the floors below. With the work complete, the family is delighted with the results and has shelved all plans to move.

# basement kitchen

Because there was a kitchen already in the basement, the young family living in this terrace house found they spent most of their time there. However, it was not ideal as the basement was a series of small, dark rooms. To open up the space and make it a useful family living area, the architect removed internal walls, fitted a beam in the ceiling and strengthened the floor to support the remaining structure. The area is now focused on the back garden with the flooring, kitchen units and refectory table lining up to run lengthways through the space, making it appear longer than it actually is.

The natural timber finishes, including that of the built-in bench on the left of the table, which forms the radiator housing, are in steamed beech. The kitchen is now streamlined and, to avoid a bulky L-shape of units running under the window, the sink is freestanding. This is the kitchen's one extravagance: the bowl is standard but the case has been made to the architect's designs. Triangular in shape, the sink is less intrusive than a rectangular or square one.

By removing internal walls and painting the room white, light has been brought right through the space. A nice touch is the back-lit splashback behind the kitchen units, which gives a great 'lift' to the cooking area.

**MAKING SPACE**

**The brief:** Revamp an existing, well-used but gloomy basement kitchen.

**The solution:** Knock down the internal walls and paint the room white to let the light permeate the whole space and help make it appear bigger than it is.

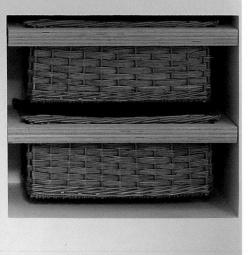

LEFT AND ABOVE **This galley kitchen design is compact but ergonomically well designed. The lighting scheme is particularly successful with twinkling ceiling-recessed lamps and the inventive detail of a back-lit splashback. There is ample storage and the bespoke sink is neat and eye-catching.**

BELOW **This is not a large space, but through clever utilization of dead, unused areas and effective streamlining, it is now able to meet the needs of its owners. The architect has succeeded in building in a lavatory with shower as well as a functional kitchen and generous dining space.**

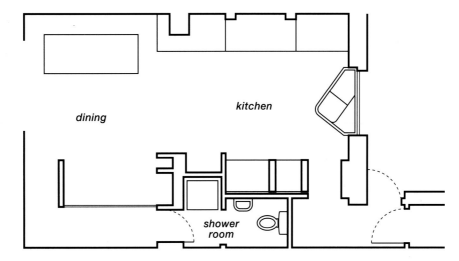

*dining*

*kitchen*

*shower room*

# minimalist basement conversion

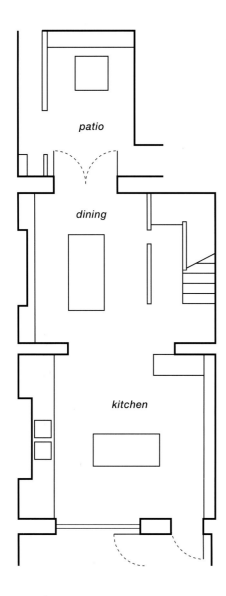

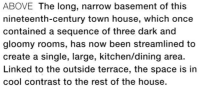

**MAKING SPACE**

ABOVE The long, narrow basement of this nineteenth-century town house, which once contained a sequence of three dark and gloomy rooms, has now been streamlined to create a single, large, kitchen/dining area. Linked to the outside terrace, the space is in cool contrast to the rest of the house.

**The brief:** To create a simple, monastic, clutter-free cooking and dining space.

**The solution:** Strip away the years of decoration, remove the partition walls and harmonize the space by painting walls white and laying a stone floor. Details are of the highest order.

The owners of this nineteenth-century town house wanted to transform their dark and cluttered basement into a single kitchen/dining room of monastic simplicity, in contrast with upstairs.

When they bought the house, it had been untouched since the 1970s. The basement floor was carved up into three rooms, which included a kitchen and bathroom, and both were decorated with wildly swirling carpets and garish wallpaper. By stripping away the gloom and paying particular attention to detail, they have made a serene, totally clutter-free space for cooking and eating.

Although the house is of some historical importance, the architect was given free rein in the basement because it had been so altered over the years and little of the original detailing remained. The layers of old flooring and decoration have been stripped away, internal walls removed and gradually the basement has been recast as a single, simple room.

The kitchen has been repositioned at the front of the house, where all the usual accoutrements of food and cooking equipment are hidden behind a wall of floor-to-ceiling doors painted cobalt blue. Throughout this single, long rectangular room, the floor is finished in pale limestone slabs and the walls are painted white. The amount of available light at the far end of the area, close to the enormous antique, chestnut refectory table, has been increased by excavating and enlarging the exterior lightwell. The limestone flooring continues through the double doors to the outside where there is a cast concrete bench, monumental table and barbecue.

Detailing in the conversion is especially fine, with bespoke stainless-steel kitchen units and a handsome staircase made with pale wood treads and risers and a steel banister. The unusual skirting throughout is a recessed band of stainless steel.

The monastic simplicity achieved was precisely what the owners had in mind at the outset and they have felt no need to introduce any extra decoration. The space now stands in cool contrast to the interiors elsewhere in the house where period detailing has survived and been restored.

LEFT The owners' antique refectory table, made of chestnut, takes pride of place in the dining area, which now opens out on to a light and airy exterior terrace.

BELOW The crisp detailing of the staircase is matched by a high-quality plaster finish on the walls, stainless-steel skirting and subtle, recessed ceiling lights.

# doing it yourself

## making changes

LEFT AND ABOVE **Coming up with your own ideas and seeing them translated into reality can be incredibly satisfying. Your project doesn't have to be enormous to be effective. This high-level glazed extension is a** real delight. It has introduced additional sunlight into the living space and has inspired a creative rooftop garden scheme to make best use of the outside area. Inside and out are separated by large sliding doors.

Following inspiration comes action. Having seen the successes achieved in the real-life projects of others, your appetite will have been whetted and no doubt you will have started to see the potential of your own home. Although the styles of properties shown in the previous pages vary enormously, the ideas are universal and can be translated to many different homes.

The final section of this book provides a practical, step-by-step guide to crystalizing your ideas and applying them to your own space. For the best results keep a sense of perspective, set clear objectives and feel confident that you are making the right changes. To achieve these goals you need to think of your home as a whole, understand how you inhabit the space and find ways of making it work harder. This approach is quite different from much of the recent advice on home improvements which rarely ventures beyond the superficial. To improve a room we have been told to add a new coat of paint, replace the upholstery, scatter some cushions or buy a new rug or lamp. But, clearly, surfaces and objects are not enough to effect a transformation. No matter how many new home-decorating tricks we learn, no matter how much we improve our eye for colour, the physical limitations of the rooms remain the same.

For many people the opportunity to make their homes as they would like them is there to be seized. Now is the time to look further than skin deep, and to swap two-dimensional thinking for three-dimensional. This is the challenge that can be met by anyone who demands more from their home.

# seeing space

A key to unlocking the full potential of any living space is to see it as an architect would. By understanding clearly how your space works, you can tailor it to fit your life more closely. When completely stripped of its furnishings and fittings the house is, in essence, a box divided into compartments. It is a highly practical structure; it provides protection from the weather, security from intruders and space in which to live and eat and rest. It is made to fit a plot of land, it is designed in a particular style, constructed using a palette of different materials and then made to function with a mass of technology.

Since few people have the opportunity to design their homes from scratch, the majority of us live in houses and flats that conform to a common set of standards. We expect to see a kitchen, living area, bathroom and bedrooms, all of which are laid out in familiar patterns – it would be a surprise to find bedrooms on the ground floor of a two-storey house. Usually such space is not tailor-made to meet our requirements and so we are obliged to fit our lives into the existing framework of rooms. Whether we like it or not, we are highly conditioned by these houses and it is a conditioning that is difficult to break. It is easy to become accustomed to the layout and its shortcomings, and ignore the fact that it is possible to change the shape, size or configuration of rooms to make them better suit the way we live.

To implement useful changes to your own space it is important to be able to look at these buildings afresh. If you live in a house then why not put the bedrooms downstairs and live upstairs if that provides you with better natural light and more flexible living space? Even small changes, such as moving a door opening or dividing a room with a counter instead of a wall, can make a big difference and it need not cost a fortune.

It can be difficult to recognize the potential of your home, and this is where the architect's skills are so important. Architects are trained to 'read' a building as a three-dimensional whole and understand how the spaces relate to each other. With a three-dimensional image in mind, it is possible to assess how a collection of interior spaces can be best arranged to meet the needs of its users. An elderly couple, for example, will make a very different set of demands on a house from a family with three teenage children.

To make your own space work most effectively, try the architect's approach: look at the whole objectively, see how the spaces relate and identify how the rooms are used.

LEFT AND RIGHT **It's difficult to see the familiar afresh; a house in daylight (right), gives away few secrets as to how the rooms relate. However, the same building at night reveals very clearly how the 'box' is divided into compartments.**

# thinking like an architect

Sketches, plans and sections are the language of the architect, but three-dimensional ideas on two-dimensional paper can take some tricky mental construction. For most of us, a model is more readily understandable. To get a real hold on the shape and room pattern of your home, try to build a three-dimensional image of it in your mind. Sketches will always be useful, but such an imaginary model should help you to see your house or flat as a whole and to visualize the impact of removing a wall, taking out ceilings or moving the staircase.

Begin the process of seeing in three dimensions by taking a cool, rational look at the building in question. It can be surprisingly difficult to stand back from your own home and see it through fresh eyes, especially if you have lived there for a while. Try to disentangle yourself from what you know about the building and strip it back to the physical essentials – a collection of compartments linked by doors, passages and stairways. Unless you have received a design education or happen to be gifted in spatial conception, this can require a large leap of the imagination. However, if you can learn to look objectively at a space, you will gain the freedom to come up with the most innovative and imaginative of ideas.

A helpful way of building this imaginary three-dimensional model is to think of the building as a doll's house. In our childhood, devising new furnishing schemes for a doll's house

is one of our earliest introductions to spatial thinking and reorganization. Imagine the front wall of your house or flat being hinged down one side, and then let it swing open to reveal how the rooms are arranged. In this way you can visualize how the stairs link floor to floor, and how the cells of space relate to each other, side by side, above and below.

In a traditional urban house the reception room will be on the ground floor at the front, with the main bedroom above. The back of the house is typically used for cooking and cleaning. But although it makes economic good sense to keep plumbing in one area, it doesn't have to be like that. Try to build a picture of your ideal room plan. With your model in mind, you'll soon get a sense of the volume of spaces enclosed by the walls and it becomes possible to play around with ideas. Imagine the drama that might be achieved by removing a ceiling and opening up a bedroom into the roof, or the effect that could be achieved by fixing a glass dome in the roof over the top of the stairs to draw a shaft of light down through the core of the building, or perhaps you'd like to take off the back of the house and build a glass extension.

LEFT **The power of the imagination: is it possible to take out a ceiling, open up the roof, slot in a glazed walkway, remove a wall and replace it with glass panels and make a first-floor sun terrace?**

# how does a space feel?

Once you are confident of the shapes and the interrelationships of the spaces you have, the next step is to look at the qualities of the overall space and decide which areas work well and which do not. What do you like and dislike? Buildings have a powerful impact on us, they can provoke the strongest responses – from making us feel oppressed and enervated to being invigorated and full of energy. For example, rooms with low ceilings can seem cosy and embracing, but if they are also small they can feel claustrophobic. Every home contains different types of space and only once you are aware of this variety can you begin to manipulate your own.

Before reshaping your own living space, it is a good idea to find real-life examples to copy or borrow from. The best way of understanding how spaces work and how rooms relate to each other is literally to walk around a variety of homes. Identify elements you like in friends' and neighbours' houses, look around homes that are up for sale, or visit historic properties. Try not to be distracted by decoration and furnishings, but focus on how you

respond to the building itself. The academic Steen Eiler Rasmussen in his book *Experiencing Architecture* suggested 'It is not enough to see architecture; you must experience it. You must dwell in the rooms, feel how they close about you, feel how you are naturally led from one to the other.' Follow Rasmussen's advice and take time to consider how you are affected by the entrance to a home – is it welcoming, forbidding or depressing? Why does it feel like that? Look critically at how you are drawn through and negotiate the

space. Are there features you particularly like – a curved wall perhaps, internal windows, or a vista through the whole space? Are there elements you really dislike – windows that are too small or doors that interfere with circulation or obscure the view on entering?

If you are remodelling a room and intend to reposition a door, think about how it will open. What will the vista be in front of you? Do you want to create a feeling of openness or do you prefer the privacy of a door that slowly reveals a room?

RIGHT **This space feels friendly, a great place for the family to eat, watch television and listen to music. We are given the strong impression that this is a fairly informal home whose occupants enjoy texture and a certain amount of visual variety. The glass partitioning, throughout, brings airiness.**

Take note of the planning and arrangement of rooms, the rhythm of the spaces, the drama of different features, the size and proportion of the rooms and the details of doors and architraving, skirting and window designs. The quality of space is also affected by the finishes used on walls, floors and furnishings. Texture and colour are powerful in affecting our responses. As you look critically at various rooms, take note of the impact of finishes: two identical apartments can have entirely separate personalities if furnished differently.

Finally, do not limit your spatial awareness to considering houses. Some of the best ideas come from the most unexpected quarters. Look more closely next time you are in the bank, it may have a beautiful granite counter; take note of smart flooring in a café, lighting in a shop... always keep your eyes and mind open.

ABOVE A more formal and exclusively adult atmosphere is created in this opened up space where a table is set for dinner and all children's toys, books and clothes are out of sight.

# reshaping your home

You are the most familiar with your home's advantages and shortcomings, and are therefore in the best position to identify where improvements can be introduced and changes can be made. By this stage you will have collected many ideas and it is time to decide which are achievable, which you would like to implement, and how the work will be done.

Undertaking any project on the home is an adventure and the rewards can be enormous, but be warned that building work is always messy and disruptive, it can be emotionally wearing and it is likely to cost substantial sums of money. Before setting out, be sure that you are doing the right thing. Work through the following considerations. Is your research thorough? Have you thought about the materials you want to use? Have you had two or three comparative quotes from suppliers, builders and so on? Can you cope with the disruption and do you have adequate funds to see the job through, including the decoration?

LEFT It's a wonderful feeling to create a home that fits you and your life. When your surroundings are comfortable, efficient, uplifting and great to live in, life really does seem a little easier.

RIGHT The mess, anxiety and chaos that are inevitable with building work should dissolve to a distant memory when you can appreciate the benefits of your new space.

# time/room analysis

As your ideas are formulating, ask yourself if you are sure that you are getting the best use out of your space. One of the many paradoxes in the way we live today is that, while the family may be crammed into one or two rooms on the ground floor for most of their waking lives, the upper part of the house (or bedrooms of the flat) often languishes empty and unused. Even in small flats, where pressure is most keenly felt, there will be 'dead' areas and rooms that can be better used. A rough floorplan sketch will help you visualize the space you have (for help in measuring up see page 150) and on to this you can note how much time is spent in different areas. Are there rooms in your house or apartment that

are empty for most of the time? An exciting and worthwhile project in any home is to reincorporate a bedroom (or two) into the daytime life of the house. A breakdown of how you spend your time might seem a complex undertaking, but it really does clarify how you occupy your home and is quite likely to produce some surprising results.

To prepare a time/room analysis, first work through an average week day, thinking through all the basic activities that you undertake. Write down the hours and the rooms in which you are occupied. Go through the same process for an average weekend day. You must then add up the total hours spent in each location over a week (multiplying the hours of an average week day by five, and of a weekend day by two). From this process you can establish the relative time spent on activities in different areas of your home. Identify the least-used areas and you can start to assess the priorities for change. Consider the tasks that you spend the most time on. Think about whether an activity could be carried out in one of the underused rooms if refinements were made to that space?

LEFT AND ABOVE LEFT **The ingenious use of a blind and sliding doors can completely close off this work area and galley kitchen and leave the room to function solely as a sitting room. An extra bedroom has been created in the space that was once occupied by a large kitchen.**

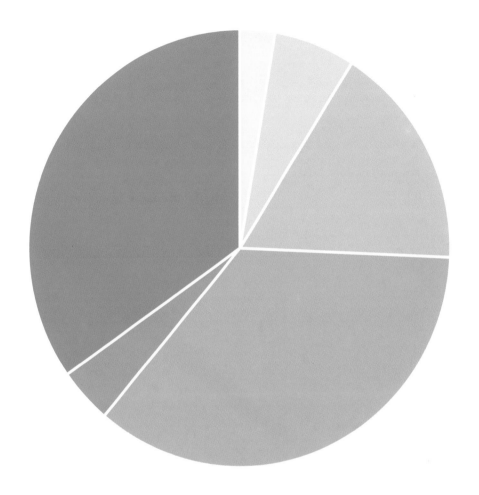

## The time analysis breakdown

| *Weekdays* | | *Weekend* | |
|---|---|---|---|
| 07.30-08.30 | Bathroom | 09.00-10.00 | Bathroom |
| 08.00-08.30 | Kitchen / Diner | 10.00-10.30 | Kitchen / Diner |
| 08.30-18.00 | Out | 10.30-12.30 | Living room |
| 18.00-19.00 | Home office (Kitchen / Diner) | 12.30-15.00 | Out |
| 19.00-19.30 | Home gym (Bedroom) | 15.00-16.00 | Home office (Kitchen / Diner) |
| 19.30-20.30 | Kitchen / Diner | 16.00-17.00 | Home gym (Bedroom) |
| 20.30-23.30 | Living room | 17.00-18.00 | Living room |
| 23.30-07.30 | Bedroom | 18.00-19.00 | Kitchen / Diner |
| | | 19.00-20.30 | Living room |
| | | 20.30-23.30 | Out |
| | | 23.30-01.30 | Living room |
| | | 01.30-09.00 | Bedroom |

bathroom ■ bedroom

kitchen/diner ■ home office

living room ■ out of the house

# assessing your needs and dreams

In addition to the time-based analysis of how you use your rooms, you should also consider the extra activities and purposes you would like a space to accommodate. You may want a place for, say, a dark room, a sound studio, a room for furniture restoration or a mini gym. Have you considered whether you would like extra accommodation for guests?

You must also think about the quality of the spaces in which you spend time doing activities. Think about aspects such as the size and the privacy of the space. How do you want a space to feel? You may, for example, only spend half an hour a day bathing, but you might consider it particularly important for your bathroom to be large and luxurious;

LEFT **If this is the home of your dreams, set yourself the goal and work towards it. Collect any pictures, magazine articles and brochures that will help you piece together your ideal space.**

or, if you enjoy the opportunity for quiet reading, you could make it a priority to build in a dedicated comfortable area within a bedroom or sitting room.

List those activities you enjoy making time for, and note the nature of the space you would like them to occupy. Do you, for example, regularly cook for friends, in which case would you like a large, fully equipped kitchen? Do you like the formality of a separate dining room? Do you prefer one large living area to smaller designated rooms?

If you are feeling adventurous, let your imagination run wild – forget the likely restrictions to be imposed by planners, conservation officers and bank managers and dream up the most outrageous ideas. Imagine stripping the entire back wall off your house, digging into the basement, moving your garden on to the roof of a new extension, or removing an entire floor and ceiling to create a double-height space. Ignore the constraints of your existing building – what would make it the ideal home?

Start with what your house or flat must provide in basic accommodation and then aim high and draw up the wish list for your dream home.

RIGHT **Don't feel inhibited by the style of an older home. Modern interventions, such as this amazing glass staircase and landing, can sit very happily within their framework.**

# case one

ABOVE To make the most of open-plan areas, some idea of structure needs to be imposed. Groups of furniture, rugs and lighting can help to define different areas and activity zones. This sofa and table create a soft living area that is quite distinct from the neat galley kitchen. This, in turn, is separated from the dining area by the counter-height divider which contains the sink and worktop.

To help you work out your own lifestyle needs and wish list, here are profiles of two households.

## Profile One

Richard is a single man in his mid-30s. He works long office hours, and enjoys playing and watching football. His basic living requirements are a bedroom, kitchen, bathroom and living room. However, as more is revealed about Richard's life, it is possible to refine this

list so that his living space can be made to enhance his lifestyle still further.

**Relationships** Richard is divorced with a daughter. His mother recently died and his father likes to visit and stay over. *A second bedroom is essential.*

**Work** This is office-based, but occasionally Richard brings home reports for rewriting. *A home office, with enough room for a computer, would be invaluable.*

**Leisure** Richard wants to keep his

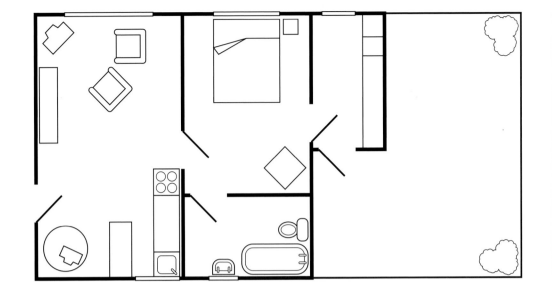

- ▷ living area with limited seating and poor definition as a relaxation zone.
- ▷ open-plan kitchen/ breakfast bar, with dining/work table.
- ▷ bedroom.
- ▷ en suite bathroom.
- ▷ utility room with door to outside, housing washing machine.
- ▷ under-utilized garden.

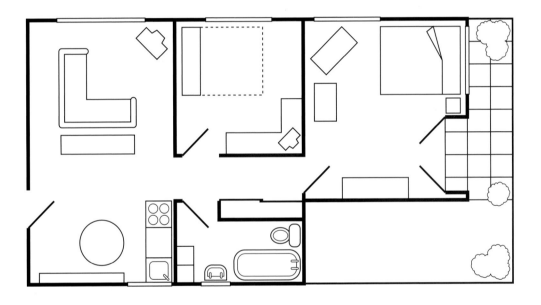

## ARCHITECT'S SOLUTION

- ▷ living area with extra seating and definition of the space.
- ▷ reduced kitchen with dining table.
- ▷ guest room/home office with work area and pull-down bed.
- ▷ smaller bathroom plumbed for washing machine.
- ▷ bedroom extension with mini gym.
- ▷ streamlined hall, running front to back, with storage facilities.
- ▷ manageable garden with patio area.

weight down and play more football. *A mini home gym would be an asset*. **Social life** Richard enjoys cooking for friends, but with long office hours he likes quick-to-prepare foods. *He needs an efficient, minimal kitchen*.

He often has friends round to watch films on a widescreen TV. *A large, soft seating area is needed*.

Richard's ideal home space would therefore need to incorporate two bedrooms (a main bedroom with

mini gym, and a guest room/home office). A living, dining, cooking space (with a large, soft seating area). A bathroom.

## The architect's solution

▷ Extend the utility space to make a main bedroom and mini gym.
▷ Reduce the old bedroom. Install a work space and pull-down bed to create a home office/guest room.
▷ Minimize the kitchen: shorten the

worktop and remove the breakfast bar. Leave the table for dining.
▷ Add extra seating to the living area and position the furniture to demarcate the space better.
▷ Narrow the bathroom and make a small hallway. Add cupboards here to increase storage and maximize space.
▷ Pave over a portion of the reduced garden to create a terrace and manageable flower beds/lawn.

# case two

ABOVE  It is a difficult task accommodating the complex needs of a family, especially when parents work from home. A successful formula is to link the kitchen with the living space. Plenty of storage space for toys is essential.

In contrast with Richard's needs, a couple with two young children, running a business from home, have a different set of requirements.

## Profile Two

Jack and Maggie run a plant nursery adjoining their house and have two children, Katie aged four and William aged seven. Their basic requirements are three bedrooms, a bathroom, a kitchen with dining area and a living room. As more is learned about the family's life, it becomes possible to tailor its needs.

**Relationships**  Jack and Maggie have

no plans to have more children. *Three bedrooms are enough.*
**Work**  Jack can get very dirty working in the nursery. *A downstairs shower room with lavatory would be extremely useful.* The nursery generates a lot of paperwork and administration. *A dedicated home office is needed.*
**Social life**  The family eats at a table in the living room, using a serving hatch to the kitchen. The couple would like to open this space, so that the children can be watched at play and there is easier kitchen access. The living area is heavily

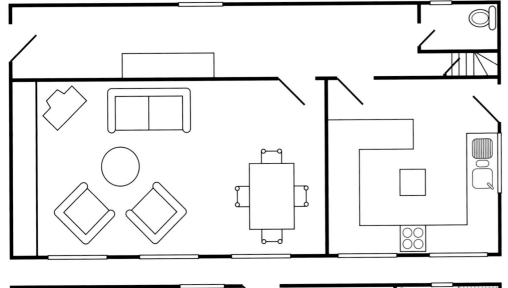

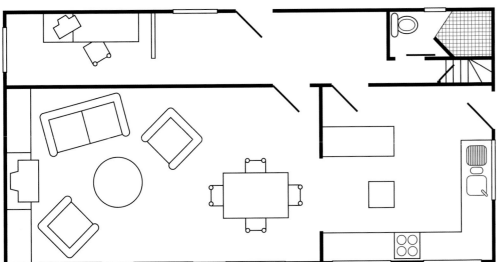

## THE STARTING POINT

▷ large living space with a dining table and a serving hatch to the kitchen.

▷ long, yet underused, hallway.

▷ large, spacious kitchen with poor access to the living space.

▷ three bedrooms.

▷ downstairs lavatory at the end of the hallway beneath the stairs.

▷ unused basement.

## ARCHITECT'S SOLUTION

▷ an efficient, traffic-free office space at the end of the hall, with stainless-steel screening in place, a relocated front door and a new window overlooking the car park.

▷ kitchen opened out to the living area.

▷ extended lavatory with tiled shower.

▷ basement converted to make a dry, soundproofed music room, installed with a piano.

family oriented with toy corners for Katie and William. *An opening needs to be made between the kitchen and living space.*
**Leisure** Maggie is a part-time piano teacher and William is learning to play. *A separate and quiet room is required for the piano.*

This family's ideal home space would therefore need to incorporate three bedrooms, a bathroom, a downstairs shower room, a separate home office, a music room, a kitchen with dining room and a living room.

### The architect's solution

▷ Use a shoulder-height, glass and stainless-steel screen to create a separate office space in the large existing hallway. Relocate the front door and make an additional window to provide views over the driveway and the customer car park.

▷ Tile the existing downstairs lavatory and install a shower unit.

▷ Join the kitchen with the living area, removing the serving hatch and part of the wall/units.

▷ Convert, damp-proof and sound-proof the basement for a music room.

# before work begins

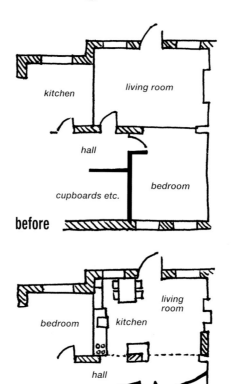

**before**

**after**

RIGHT AND BELOW This one-bedroom flat has undergone some major reshaping to create a three-bedroom home. Because the family spent most of its time in the small kitchen, it was decided to move the kitchen into the living room. The former kitchen has become a bedroom, the living room now opens out into the hall and the large bedroom has been slightly reduced in size to provide room for a run of large cupboards in the hall. The tangle of old cupboards, bathroom and loo have been reorganized to make a small bathroom and bedroom. The family now has a great, open, kitchen living space, (below), that exactly suits its needs.

FAR RIGHT The smallest bedroom is compact, but is so well planned and organized that there is even room for a tiny home office.

## Planning

Along with gathering and formulating ideas, undertaking a building project involves good planning. There are some practical considerations before work can begin.

## Making sketches

Make sketches of several different floorplan layouts, and imagine what these would be like to live in. How would the changes affect, improve and enliven your current space? Do they answer all your requirements? You should consider whether the changes will add value to the property. Beware of making them so idiosyncratic that no one will buy it from you.

## Construction and materials

When it comes to deciding just how to shape your space, do some basic research into the way your home is

constructed. Solid internal walls may be holding up ceilings and are therefore more tricky to remove than partition walls. To find out what sort of walls you have, knock them – a simple partition will make a hollow sound.

Consider the scale and size of the house – a 20-metre- (65-foot-) long extension might look fine on an enormous home, but it is likely to look ludicrous on a modest two-storey suburban house. The scale and design of internal fittings should also suit the size of your home.

As you piece together your ideas, think about the palette of materials you would like to use. Do not feel obliged to choose materials that imitate or are an exact match of those already used elsewhere in your home. The introduction of a new material into an existing building can add excitement – a slab of glistening white concrete, etched glass, glass bricks, or a partition of riveted steel can look stunning alongside the traditional materials of brick or stone. Be careful not to write off anything. You might think you dislike concrete, but once you see the latest finishes achieved using this most versatile of materials, you could find that you change your mind. Whatever you choose, make sure that it is of the best possible quality you can afford and that it is finished well.

Ecological concerns may well play a part in your decisions. The construction industry has grown more aware of its environmental responsibilities than it was a decade ago. When it comes to traditional building materials it is now possible to gain details of their green credentials. When using timber, for example, check that it is from a sustainable and well-managed source. It is also possible to find out what sorts of preservatives and anti-rot chemicals have been used. If you want to use untreated wood, consult with your architect and/or builder. Using recycled and salvaged materials may be an option too. Buying local materials will reduce the cost and pollution that can be caused by transportation.

# limitations and priorities

## Budget estimates

An important question to be asked at this stage concerns finance – do you have an adequate amount of money to spend? Do you know the maximum you can borrow and the maximum you can actually afford to borrow? Set yourself a limit for the scheme's budget and stick to it. Build in a ten per cent buffer zone – it is comforting when the unexpected happens, and a bonus if it doesn't. Here are the main expenses to consider.

- Builder's quote – including all materials.
- Plumber, electrician, gas fitter fees.
- Architect's fees.
- Planning fees.
- Fixtures and fittings that you will have to buy, e.g. bathroom suite, doors, windows.
- Decorating costs, including flooring.
- Ten per cent buffer.

## Budget reviews

If you are planning major work and it is beyond your initial budget, could the job be completed in stages? Do you need to be so radical? If it is within budget, could you be more radical?

## Building restrictions

An essential piece of research is to discover whether your home is subject to any planning or conservation restrictions. If your property is registered as being of historic interest, it is likely that you will be unable to remove walls or tamper with internal detailing such as cornices or fireplaces. You will also need to seek permission for even fairly simple schemes like making or moving a doorway. However, there are clever ways of working around these restrictions – for example, in one listed house even the ceramic floor tiles were listed for preservation, but the owners wanted a wooden floor. The solution was to keep the tiles and lay the timber floor over the top.

You may find that there are restrictions imposed by law on the sorts of materials that you can use in your scheme, the shapes and types of replacement windows and even the colour you paint the exterior. However, in addition to preserving the past, a small number of planning authorities are prepared to keep an open mind when it comes to adding extensions to protected buildings. If the proposed structure is of a high-quality design and uses elegant materials, it is possible that your architect will be successful in arguing his or her case.

## Building plan reviews

If you are unlucky enough to have your plans turned down and you think your proposals are reasonable, it is essential that you talk with your planning department. It may be that you have been turned down on a technicality, in which case you will need to get to the root of the problems and resubmit your proposals. To avoid this anxiety and time loss, it is a good idea to consult your local planners before you submit an application as they can offer advice on sensitive issues.

LEFT You might think that gaining permission for such a daring glass extension would be problematic, but time spent with planners will help you negotiate the minefield of local planning law. Plenty of councils are open-minded and willing to encourage good-quality modern design.

ABOVE Some really exciting results can be achieved when you are prepared to push at the boundaries. Sometimes plans are refused because of a small technicality that could easily be overcome. Consultation is always worthwhile. Even planners don't expect us all to live in the past.

# understanding plans

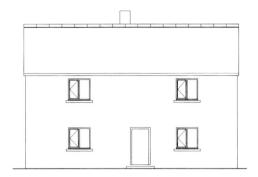

• The Elevation
Plans can at first appear intimidating, but learning how to interpret them can be a tremendous asset when dealing with architects. These are two simple elevations – the top drawing shows a front elevation and the lower drawing shows a side elevation.

Before any work can begin, a set of plans is an essential requirement. Even where the job is small, it is worth having the extra security of a paper-based design to work from. If, for example, your builder moves a window just 20 centimetres (8 inches) too far to the right, it could completely ruin your vision of the space; or, if you had designed the room around a piece of furniture and found that, through just a small mistake, it no longer fitted where intended, it might be the ruin of your dream. Imagine the potential disasters in a larger and more complex job. If the measurements are clearly marked on plans there is no room for misunderstanding or argument.

Most people are unfamiliar with looking at and reading plans. At first glance the intricate web of lines can seem rather daunting, but in most domestic projects the plans should be easy to follow. Once you have found a major element like the front door, it should be fairly straightforward to orient yourself.

At this stage you will have started experimenting with sketches and rough plans to check that your ideas work. Software programmes are available to help you experiment with layouts and change the dimensions of your space. These are enjoyable to play around with and enable you to print out the results, but whether you choose paper or computer to realize your ideas, you will still need to measure the rooms.

Measuring sounds such a simple task, but if done badly it can wreak havoc. If you decide to use the services of an architect, he or she will conduct a full measured survey of the property. However your own measurements will still help you formulate ideas and discard the impossible.

There are two basic types of architectural drawings: the three dimensional and the two dimensional. The former is more difficult for the unskilled to draw, but offers the best outline visualization of the space. Two-dimensional drawings come in three basic types: the floorplan (looking at the floor layout from above), the cross-section (looking at a slice of the inside of the building from the side), and the elevation (looking at a view of the exterior). To gain an idea about how your project might work, you will probably only need floorplans to start with. Here the building is sliced through horizontally so you can see where the doors and windows feature, and how the spaces are divided by walls. Once you have drawn the basic layout keep this as a master, and use photocopies to allow you to experiment with different schemes. To give an idea of scale you might draw in some of the larger items of furniture such as the sofa, dining table and bed.

Files are invaluable for keeping together your early ideas. As well as holding the growing numbers of sketches and drawings, they can also contain magazine cuttings, leaflets and brochures from suppliers.

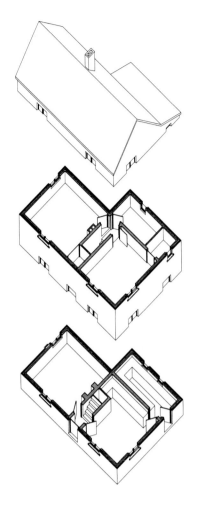

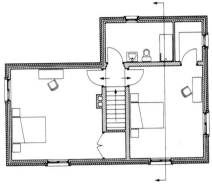

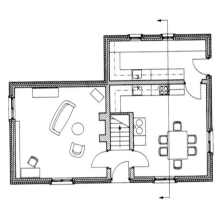

• The Floor Plan
The two drawings, immediately on the left and below, are floorplans. They show the positions of walls, stairs, windows, doors and furniture. They relate directly to the dissected 3-D house on the far left.

*first floor*

*ground floor*

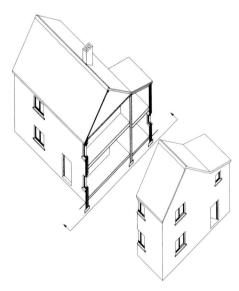

• The Cross Section
This is a cross-section drawing at the point indicated by the arrows on the floorplans, above, and the 3-D image, shown far left. As the name suggests, a cross-section shows a view of a house, looking through it vertically.

# measuring up

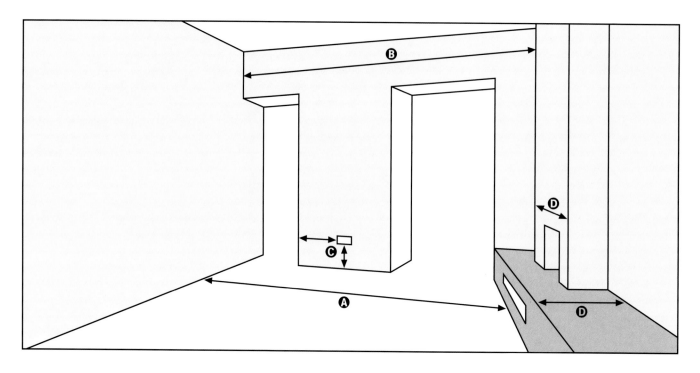

ABOVE **No time is ever wasted on measuring. This provides the basis on which you can make your plans and feel confident when ordering materials or furniture.**

It is advisable to measure and note just about everything that stands still – not only the length and height of the walls, but, if possible, their thickness too. Measure the precise locations of doors and windows – measuring to the outside of the frames, and distances from floors and ceilings. It is a good idea to mark in electrical sockets and light switches, as well as radiators, pipes, telephone sockets and the locations of any underfloor services. If you know any construction details like the direction of floor joists, make a note of these too.

**Ⓐ Floor** Use the longest tape-measure you can find. The usual, small-size measures tend to be around 2 metres (7 feet) in length, which is incredibly annoying when measuring rooms, which are inevitably larger than that.

When starting to measure a floor it's a good idea to have a rough sketch of the room. As you measure, note down the lengths. You can draw the plan to scale later. Key floor measurements are the length and width, but diagonal measurements are also useful when rooms are not perfectly symmetrical. Note the direction of floorboards and joists (which run at 90 degrees to the boards) on your plan.

**Ⓑ Walls** Here you'll be measuring the elevation, the height and width of walls, the positions of windows and doors, the curtain rails, skirting board and cornicing. Because the walls are likely to be different, you'll need a separate sketch and set of measurements for each. It may also be useful to measure the diagonals again here, at about 1 metre (3 feet) above the floor level.

**◉ Power points and switches** These are precisely the sorts of details that you will find really important when it comes to reshaping rooms. If you think they are in an awkward position now, remember to make a note on the plan to get this changed during the course of the work.

**◉ Features** Of vital importance on plans are all the room's features. No detail is too small. Make a note of the cupboards, radiators, chimney-breasts, alcoves, radiators, and even register on which side of the doors the hinges are.

When it comes to drawing up plans to scale, it is advisable to use graph paper and then set yourself a scale: this depends on the paper of course, but, for example, it could be a ratio of 1 square to 25 millimetres (1 inch).

ABOVE **Many rooms can contain a number of optical illusions, so don't rely on rough estimates when you are describing the dimensions of your rooms. You may find that windows do not line up with one another or that doorways prove too small to allow in larger pieces of furniture.**

# working with architects and builders

removed from the reality – architects would simply not survive in business if clients were treated with such disdain.

The truth is that, as in all professions, there are still some bad architects who want to follow their own agenda, but the majority of practitioners are reasonable and talented professionals. They are daily confronted by the challenges of making space work and have amassed invaluable experience in

ABOVE **Architects are tremendously skilled at assessing problems and devising inventive solutions. This dark hall was made light through the replacement of a solid wall with a sandblasted glass screen. The wall now has a luminous quality whether it is lit by natural daylight or ceiling-recessed halogen lamps.**

During the past few decades architects have earned themselves an unfortunate reputation. The stereotypical image is of arrogant artists who are so determined to pursue their own vision that they are deaf to the requests of the client; they will run away with your budget and produce an unlovable and unliveable design with slabs of glass, steel and concrete. Fortunately this image is far solving problems, dealing with planners and builders and specifying materials. They are able to transform spaces with the simplest of solutions and find a number of exciting products. Architects can also produce excellent value for money, and can even save money by knowing about salvaged materials or little-known sources of obscure grants.

Despite this you need to make sure that you find an architect that suits your needs and your project. Inviting a complete stranger to help you reshape your home is an emotionally charged business. The stakes are high and there is no room for a rash gamble. Get this wrong and an important project will be turned to misery.

The first step to success is not to rush. Be sure that making changes, adding an extension, expanding into the roof or excavating the basement is what you want to do.

BELOW Many architects and designers are fascinated by materials and products. They can be a fund of information on intriguing lighting, flooring, countertop surfaces, window frames and all sorts of wall finishes. The most appealing new products are drawn from unlikely sources such as laboratory design and retail projects.

Although you will start to form ideas about what you want to achieve, be prepared to keep an open mind. However, if your heart is set on a piece of design or a particular feature don't let an architect or designer dissuade you. Never allow them to impose their own ideas if you disagree – always remember that you are the client and you are paying.

When you are ready to find a design professional who can translate your sketches and cuttings into a three-dimensional reality, there are various experts you can call upon. If you are confident about your own building, technical and negotiating skills you might simply need someone to prepare a set of drawings for submission to the planning authority. Alternatively, you may opt to employ someone who can help you through the whole process to completion.

In these early stages, time spent on research is never wasted. Whether you are reshaping or extending a property, begin your search for an architect or designer by telephoning their professional body.

Draw up a short list of between three and six people or companies to approach. Take along your sketchpad of ideas, your budget and your timescale to discuss. Show them your ideas and ask their opinion. Within the first hour of meeting you will probably know whether you will get on. If they don't show you photographs of previous projects (a bad sign) then ask to see some. Ask about fees, how

your budget will be handled, whether the architect thinks the money is adequate, whether there will be problems with planning permission and when, realistically, you can expect the job to be finished. Even though you may know the best builder in the world, do allow your architect to offer the work to tender and get your builder to make a competitive bid. You may be pleasantly surprised at the results. Always be truthful. If you don't like something, say so. If you are working to an extremely tight budget tell the architect at the start, and never be afraid to ask questions. If you don't understand the plans, say so.

If you feel good about this architect or designer, take your research one step further. Visit previous projects, talk to the clients, find out whether the architect was good at listening to suggestions, keeping the client informed and so on. If you are undertaking the project with a partner or friend make sure you are in complete agreement – if not, you'll only be storing up trouble for yourself later should anything go wrong. Ask yourself whether you are confident of the architect's abilities, happy with the fees, and sure that communication will be clear and efficient. Be positive that you like them (it's a good test to ask yourself whether you'd be happy to go for lunch or a drink with them) and, above all, ask yourself if you are absolutely convinced that you'll get the results you want. If the answers are all yes, then it is time to begin.

In choosing a builder, take the same approach as in choosing an architect. You are letting these people into your home, you'll have to talk with them and negotiate with them over weeks or months. You certainly need to feel happy that you have a good rapport.

Your architect should suggest two or three firms, but you might like to find a couple independently too. There is likely to be an open tender process, which means that the architect prepares a schedule of works listing what is to be done and the builder will then offer a quote for the job.

LEFT AND BELOW  In creating the home of your dreams, don't make any rushed decisions. Spend plenty of time on researching your ideas and always ask lots of questions. Take every opportunity to visit showrooms and as many newly completed projects as possible.

The cheapest quote is not necessarily the best, so remember to check the quality and approach of the builder: go and visit previous jobs, talk to clients. If you cannot stand loud radio music or a lack of punctuality, now is the time to find out if their habits will drive you crazy. Ask if they were considerate in cleaning up and moving furniture out of harm's way. Were the contractors friendly and courteous, and were they completely trustworthy and reliable? Make sure your mind is fully at ease before signing any paperwork.

# address book

**Andrée Putman**
Sarl 83
Avenue Denfert-Rochereau
Paris 75014
France
tel: 33 1 5542 8855

**Annie Gregson**
25 Cleveland Terrace
London W2 6QH
tel: 44 207 262 4386

**Antonio Citterio**
Via Lovanio, 8
Milan 20121
Italy
tel: 39 2 655 5902

**Arthur Collin Architect**
1a Berry Place
London EC1V 0JD
tel: 44 207 490 3520

**Arturo Cogolo**
c/o Usick Heal
37 Grafton Way
London W1P 5LA
tel: 44 207 383 2000

**Ash Sakula Architects**
38 Mount Pleasant
London WC1X 0AN
tel: 44 207 837 9735

**Axel Verhoustraeten**
12 Place du jardin du fleurs
Brussels 1000
Belgium
tel: 32 2 511 4038

**Azman Owens Architects**
8 St Albans Place
London N1 0NX
tel: 44 207 354 2955

**Bere: Architects**
24 Rosebery Avenue
London EC1R 4RR
tel: 44 207 837 9333

**Cantrell & Crowley**
Architects & Interior Designers
118 Rock Road
Booterstown
Co. Dublin
Ireland
tel: 353 1 283 2055

**Carlo Seminck**
c/o Arcas Group
Natiënlaan 75a
Knokke-Heist 8300
Belgium
tel: 32 5 062 0300

**Carter Reynolds**
155 Upper Street
London N1 1RA
tel: 44 207 354 5403

**Christian Liaigre**
61 rue de Varenne
75007 Paris
France
tel: 33 1 4753 7876

**Claire Bataille & Paul Ibens**
Vekestraat 13 Bus 14
Antwerpen 2000
Belgium
tel: 32 3 213 8620

**Dale Loth Architects**
1 Cliff Road
London NW1 9AJ
tel: 44 207 485 4003

**David Chipperfield Architects**
1a Cobham Mews
Agar Grove
London NW1 9SB
tel: 44 207 267 9422

**David Mikhail Architects**
68–74 Rochester Place
London NW1 9JX
tel: 44 207 485 4696

**De Metz Green Architects**
Unit 4
250 Finchley Road
London NW3 6DN
tel: 44 207 435 1144

**Dols Wong Architects**
Loft 3
329 Harrow Road
London W9 3RB
tel: 44 207 266 2129

**Form Design Architecture**
1 Bermondsey Exchange
179–181 Bermondsey Street
London SE1 3UW
tel: 44 207 407 3336

**Haworth Tompkins Architects**
19/20 Great Sutton Street
London EC1V 0DN
tel: 44 207 250 3225

**Hudson Featherstone**
49–59 Old Street
London EC1V 9HX
tel: 44 207 490 5656

**Hugh Broughton Architects**
4 Addison Bridge Place
London W14 8XP
tel: 44 207 602 8840

**James Lambert Architects**
5 St John Street
London EC1M 4AA
tel: 44 207 608 0833

**Jo Crepain**
Vlaanderenstraat 6
Antwerpen 2000
Belgium
tel: 32 3 213 6162

**John Pardy**
The Studio
Eastwoods
Ridgeway Lane
Lymington
Hampshire SO41 8AA
tel: 44 1590 677226

**John Pawson**
Unit B
70–78 York Way
London N1 9AG
tel: 44 207 837 2929

**John Wardle Architects**

25 William Street

Richmond

Victoria 3121

Australia

tel: 61 3 9421 0700

**Keith Cunningham**

174 High Street

Edinburgh EH1 1QS

tel: 44 131 225 7555

**Littman Goddard Hogarth**

12 Chelsea Wharf

London SW10 0QJ

tel: 44 207 351 7871

**Mark Guard**

161 Whitfield Street

London W1P 5RY

tel: 44 207 380 1199

**Martin Wagner Architect**

Piazza della Costa

CH 6914 Carona

Switzerland

tel: 41 91 649 9089

**McDonnell Associates Ltd**

104 New Bond Street

London W1Y 9LG

tel: 44 207 242 1810

**McDowell + Benedetti**

62 Rosebery Avenue

London EC1R 4RR

tel: 44 207 278 8810

**Michael Squires & Partners**

8 Cromwell Place

London SW7 2JN

tel: 44 207 581 9000

**Nicholas Gioia**

297 Rae Street

North Fitzroy

Victoria 3068

Australia

tel: 61 3 9482 4555

**Nick Hockley**

ORMS

1 Pine Street

London EC1R 0JH

tel: 44 207 833 8533

**Peter Bernamont**

Wharf Studios

Baldwin Terrace

London N1 7RU

tel: 44 207 704 6859

**Rick Mather Architects**

123 Camden High Street

London NW1 7JR

tel: 44 207 284 1727

**Roland Cowan Architects**

99 Westbourne Park Villas

London W2 5ED

tel: 44 207 229 5599

**Simon Conder Associates**

Nile Street Studios

8 Nile Street

London N1 7RF

tel: 44 207 251 2144

**Snell Associates**

50b Abbey Gardens

St John's Wood

London NW8 9AT

tel: 44 207 328 6593

**Stanton Williams Architect**

Diespeker Wharf

38 Graham Street

London N1 8JG

tel: 44 207 880 6400

**Tugman Partnership**

51a George Street

Richmond

Surrey

TW9 1HJ

tel: 44 208 332 2885

**Urban Salon**

Studio 32

No.1 Chink Street

London SE1 9DG

tel: 44 207 357 8800

**Wim Depuydt**

Niewwevaart 118 Bus 2

Gent 9000

Belgium

tel: 32 9 233 7154

**Woolf Architect**

39–51 Highgate Road

London NW5 1RT

tel: 44 207 428 9500

*Other useful addresses:*

**Bund Deutscher Architekten**

14b Ippendorfer Allee

Bonn 53127

Germany

tel: 49 228 2850 11

**Japan Institute of Architects**

JIA Kan

2–3–18 Jingurmae

Shibuya-ka

Tokyo 150-001

Japan

tel: 81 6 689 6009

**Royal Australian Institute of Architects**

PO Box 3373

Red Hill

Manuka

Canberra

tel: 61 2 6273 1548

**Royal Institute of British Architects**

66 Portland Place

London W1N 4AD

tel: 44 207 307 3700

**South Africa Institute of Architects**

Private Bag x10063

Randburg 2125

South Africa

tel: 27 11 886 9349

# index

# acknowledgements

The publisher thanks the following photographers and architects for their kind permission to reproduce the photographs in this book:

**1** Verne Fotografie (arch: Jo Crepain) **2-3** Hamish Park (James Lambert Architects) **4-5** Richard Waite (Littman Goddard Hogarth Architects) **6-7** Jan Verlinde (arch: Carlo Seminck) **8** Archipress (arch: Le Corbusier) **9** Belle Magazine **10-11** Mark Fiennes (arch: Charles Rennie Mackintosh) **11 right** Henry Wilson (arch: Mark Guard) **12** Peter Cook/View (arch: Frank Lloyd Wright) **13** Chris Gascoigne/View (arch: Nick Hockley) **14 left** Grazia Branco/IKETRADE (des: Ross Lovegrove) **14-15** Jonathan Pilkington/Living etc/ipc magazines (arch: Urban Salon) **16** Corbis Bettman **17** Simon Kenny/ Belle Magazine (des: Sue Serle) **18** Richard Waite **19** Guy Obijn **20** Jan Verlinde (des: Leo Aerts for Alinea) **21** Paul Ryan/International Interiors (des: Christain Liaigre) **22** Richard Davies (arch: Snell Associates) **24 left** Dennis Gilbert/View (arch: James Melvin & Gollin Melvin Ward & Partners) **24-25** Paul Warchol (arch: Francoise DeMenil) **25 right** Mark Daley/Esto (arch: Stanley Saitowitz) **26** Verne Fotografie (arch: Wim Depuydt) **27** Rodney Weidland/Vogue Living (arch: Michael Rigg) **28** Henry Wilson/The Interior Archive (arch: David Mikhail) **29** Hamish Park (arch: James Lambert Architects) **30-31** Jan Verlinde (arch: Luk Reyn) **32** Carlos Dominguez (des: McDonnell Associates Ltd) **33** Jan Verlinde (arch: Geert Driesen) **34 left** Christian Sarramon **34-35** Keith Collie (Azman Owen Architects) **36** Andy Keate & Sussie Ahlburg (Ash Sakula Architects) **36-37** Peter Cook/View (arch: Tugman Partnership) **38-39** John Glover (arch: John Pawson) **40 above** Richard Waite **40 below** Michel Claus **41** Ray Main/Mainstream **42 left** Reiner Blunck (arch: Ray Kappe) **42 below centre** Trevor Mein/Belle Magazine/Arcaid (arch: Sean Godsell) **42-43** Richard Bryant/Arcaid (arch: John Pardy) **43 left** Reiner Blunck (arch: Ray Kappe) **43 right** Reiner Blunck (arch: Mark Mack) **44 left** Ed Reeve (arch: De Metz Green) **44-45** Ray Main/Mainstream **45 right** Ray Main/Mainstream (des: Laurence Llewelyn-Bowen) **47** Richard Bryant/Arcaid (arch: Rick Mather) **48-49** Grazia Branco/IKETRADE (arch: Dols Wong Architects) **50 left** Richard Glover (Ash Sakula Architects) **50-51** Chris Gascoigne/View (arch: Stanton Williams) **51 right** Jan Verlinde (arch: Gert Cuypers) **52-53** Henry Wilson/The Interior Archive (arch: Mark Guard) **53 right** Paul Ryan/International Interiors (des: Lee Mindel) **54** Peter Cook/View (arch: Tugman Patnership) **55 above** Tim Beddow/The Interior Archive (arch: Cantrell + Crowley) **55 below** Dennis Gilbert/View (arch: Gollin Melvin Ward & Partners) **56 left** Verne Fotografie (arch: Wim Depuydt) **56-57** Vaclav Sedy/Casabella (arch: Tod Williams Billie Tsien & Associates) **58** Verne Fotografie (Gallia Solomonof) **59** Verne Fotografie (arch: Axel Verhoustraeten) **60** Richard Glover (arch: Annie Gregson) **61** arch: Urban Splash Ltd. **62** Eduard Hueber (arch: Marble Fairbanks Architects)

**63** Petrina Tinsley/Belle Magazine **64 left** Richard Bryant/Arcaid (arch: David Chipperfield) **64-65** Andrea Zani **65 right** Trevor Mein/Arcaid (arch: John Wardle Architects) **66 left** Christopher Boas **66-67** Reiner Blunck (arch: Martin Wagner) **68-69** David Grandorge (arch: Hudson Featherstone) **70** Esto (arch: James Bischoff) **73-75** Form Design Architecture **76 left** Carter Reynolds **77-79** Ray Main/Mainstream (arch: Carter Reynolds) **80** Dale Loth Architects **81** Richard Glover/Conran Octopus (Dale Loth Architects) **82-83** arch: Peter Bernamont **84-85** Tim Beddow/The Interior Archive (des: O'Hagan) **85** Lucus Allen/Vogue Living (arch: Kerstin Thompson) **86-89** Belle Magazine (arch: Nicholas Giola) **90-91** Jan Verlinde (Claire Bataille & Paul Ibens Design N.V.) **92** Azman Owen Architects **93-95** Paul Ratigan (Azman Owen Architects) **96-97** Peter Cook/View (arch: Michael Squires & Partners) **98-99** Matthew Weinreb (Woolf Architects) **100** Ed Reeve (Littman Goddard Hogarth Architects) **101** Littman Goddard Hogarth Architects **102-103** Ed Reeve (Littman Goddard Hogarth Architects) **104-105** Ray Main/Mainstream (arch: Arturo Cogollo) **106-107** Marcus Hilton (Roland Cowen Architects) **108-111** Deidi von Schaewen (arch: Andrée Putman) **112** Carlos Dominguez (arch: McDonnel Associates Ltd) **113** Jeremy Cockayne/Arcaid (arch: Corin Mellor) **114-115** BO BEDRE **116-117** Tim Hawkins (Littman Goddard Hogarth Architects) **118-121** Richard Glover/Conran Octopus (Azman Owen Architects) **122-123** Kim Sayer/Homes & Gardens/Robert Harding Syndication (Littman Goddard Hogarth Architects) **124-125** Keith Collie (Azman Owen Architects) **126-127** Nicholas Kane/Arcaid (Ash Sakula Architects) **128-129** Andy Chopping (Haworth Tompkins Architects) **130-131** Fabrizio Bergamo/Studio Collage/B&B Italia (arch: Antonio Citterio) **132** Mark Burgin/Arcaid (arch: Jeremy Salmon) **133** Hamish Park (James Lambert Architects) **134** Ray Main/Mainstream **135** Chris Tubbs/Living etc/ipc magazines (arch:Keith Cunningham) **136** Carlos Dominguez (Hugh Broughton Architects) **138** Lizzie Himmel (arch: Deamer Phillips) **139** Grazia Branco/IKETRADE (Dols Wong Architects) **142** Simon Brown/Conran Octopus **144-145** Nicholas Kane/Arcaid (Ash Sakula Architects) **146-147** Michael Hayward/Bere Architects **147 right** Peter Cook/View (Tugman Partnership) **148-149** Diagrams: *Understanding Plans*, Peter Murray & Michelle Ogundehin, published by Wordsearch **151** Richard Glover (arch: John Pawson) **152 left** Tim Soar (arch: McDowel & Beneditti) **153-155 above** Richard Glover (Arthur Collins Architects) **155 below** Richard Waite (arch/des:Philip Billingham & Heidi Wish)

*Every effort has been made to trace the copyright holders, architects and designers and we apologise in advance for any unintentional omission and would be pleased to insert the appropriate acknowledgement in any subsequent editions.*